Managing Children's Homes

other titles in the series

Costs and Outcomes in Children's Social Care
Messages from Research
Jennifer Beecham and Ian Sinclair
Foreword by Parmjit Dhanda MP
ISBN 978 1 84310 496 4

of related interest

Residential Child Care
Prospects and Challenges
Edited by Andrew Kendrick
ISBN 978 1 84310 526 8

Improving Children's Services Networks
Lessons from Family Centres
Jane Tunstill, Jane Aldgate and Marilyn Hughes
ISBN 978 1 84310 461 2

Enhancing Social Work Management
Theory and Best Practice from the UK and USA
Edited by Jane Aldgate, Lynne Healy, Barris Malcolm, Barbara Pine,
Wendy Rose and Janet Seden
ISBN 978 1 84310 515 2

Enhancing the Well-being of Children and Families
through Effective Interventions
International Evidence for Practice
Edited by Colette McAuley, Peter J. Pecora and Wendy Rose
Foreword by Maria Eagle MP
ISBN 978 1 84310 116 1

The Pursuit of Permanence
A Study of the English Child Care System
Ian Sinclair, Claire Baker, Jenny Lee and Ian Gibbs
ISBN 978 1 84310 595 4

Fostering Now
Messages from Research
Ian Sinclair
Foreword by Tom Jeffreys
ISBN 978 1 84310 362 2

Managing Children's Homes

Developing Effective Leadership in Small Organisations

Leslie Hicks, Ian Gibbs, Helen Weatherly and Sarah Byford

Jessica Kingsley Publishers
London and Philadelphia

First published in 2007
by Jessica Kingsley Publishers
116 Pentonville Road
London N1 9JB, UK
and
400 Market Street, Suite 400
Philadelphia, PA 19106, USA

www.jkp.com

Library of Congress Cataloging in Publication Data
Managing children's homes : developing effective leadership in small organizations /
Leslie Hicks ... [et al.].
    p. cm.
Includes bibliographical references and index.
    ISBN-13: 978-1-84310-542-8 (alk. paper) 1. Group homes for children--Great
Britain--Management. 2. Children--Institutional care--Great Britain. 3. Social work
administration--Great Britain. 4. Leadership. I. Hicks, Leslie.
    HV866.G7.M36 2008
    326.73'2068--dc22

                                                    2007022558

British Library Cataloguing in Publication Data
A CIP catalogue record for this book is available from the British Library

ISBN 978 1 84310 542 8

Printed and bound in Great Britain by
Athenaeum Press, Gateshead, Tyne and Wear

For those who have looked after us

Contents

List of Tables and Figures

Acknowledgements

The research on which this book draws was achieved on the basis of goodwill and co-operation from many people, all of whom deserve our gratitude and thanks.

Those who took part directly by providing information formed the mainstay of the project. Participants were from 13 different organisations with responsibilities for providing residential care for children and young people. These included managers of children's homes, residential staff, young people and their field social workers, and those responsible for finance and accountancy. The senior managers who acted as liaison officers were especially important in enabling us to achieve the levels of response needed for a successful project. No one was blessed with extra time to incorporate research into their practice or management of it; we were stimulated by the efforts and enthusiasm that participants showed for the project.

In-house, we have valued contributions from many sources. Clerical and research assistance were provided cheerfully and efficiently by Sarah Clark, Anne Thompson and Beverley Mills. The extensive transcription work was carried out with speed, accuracy and good spirits by Sara Christensen. Penny Williams, Wendy Allison and Claire Baker shared in carrying out fieldwork, as did our late and greatly missed colleague, Lesley Archer, whose insight into practice was, and is, an abiding influence. At an analytical level, our statistical abilities have been strengthened by the expertise and patience of Nigel Rice from the Centre for Health Economics at the University of York. A special role has been occupied by Ian Sinclair, who has unfailingly provided constructive criticism, advice and expert opinion.

We have also benefited greatly from the contributions made by our Advisory Group members, who were committed particularly to ensuring that this research should be used to positive effect. We have also drawn on advice from and discussions with colleagues funded under the same Department of Health research initiative, 'The Costs and Effectiveness of Services to Children in Need'. Our final acknowledgement is to our funders, the Department of Health (responsibility for this research has since transferred to the Department for Children, Schools and Families), and to those within the Department who provided support, encouragement and information throughout, particularly Carolyn Davies, Caroline Thomas and Mark Burrows.

Leslie Hicks
Ian Gibbs
Helen Weatherly
Sarah Byford

Note on changes to the structure of government departments in June 2007

In the course of writing this book three new government departments were set up by the Prime Minister on 28 June 2007:

- The Department for Children, Schools and Families (DCSF)
- The Department for Innovation, Universities and Skills (DIUS)

These new departments replaced the Department for Education and Skills (DfES).

The Department for Children, Schools and Families (DCSF) is responsible for improving the focus on all aspects of policy affecting children and young people.

Chapter 1

Introduction and Background

Introduction

This book is about the internal management of children's homes. It focuses on the role of managers, the kinds of leadership in operation in homes, the way resources are used, and the care and outcomes experienced by young people.

Residential care is an important part in the continuum of services for children in need (Department of Health 1998). In England and Wales this provision has been fraught with difficulties in recent years, and there are many hypotheses about how these might be reduced. Problems of expense, scandal and abuse, disorder and lack of effectiveness have been extensively documented in inquiries and overviews (for example, Colton 2002; Kirkwood 1993; Stein 2006; Utting 1997). There have been drastic cuts in the number of residential homes and this in turn apparently has increased the difficulty and costs of running them. The smaller number of homes care for the most damaged adolescents (Berridge and Brodie 1998). Staffing ratios and hence costs have been increased to manage the situation. Staff turnover has increased thus raising the difficulty of creating a coherent culture in establishments where most residents stay only for a short time. Homes have found it increasingly difficult to specialise and define clear aims for themselves. In sum, children's homes now cater for a diverse population of adolescents with complex histories. This is done at high cost and a high risk of disturbance.

Despite these difficulties it is hard to envisage a world that does not use residential care as a resource to protect and develop young people. Residential provision plays a major part in relation to social inclusion (Kendrick 2005), particularly for adolescents – in preparation for placements in foster care, in preparation for adulthood, in providing supported accommodation – and for those who make a later entry to the care system, such as unaccompanied asylum-seeking young people. Residential care is also used to provide short-term care to support families under stress (Crimmens and Milligan 2005) and research suggests that increasing numbers of children with disabilities are entering residential care at an early age (Clough, Bullock and Ward 2006). Residential options offer both consistency and creative potential within children's services.

These vital functions are set within broader contexts. The number of teenagers in the general population is rising. Professional opinion, as articulated in the Utting report (1997), accepts the case for residential care. Some 'looked after' children (i.e. those for whom local authorities share or have parental responsibility, as defined in the Children Act 1989) undoubtedly prefer residential care to foster care (Sinclair and Gibbs 1998a; Utting 1991). Foster care places for teenagers are scarce (Waterhouse 1997). Pressures on local authorities to reduce turnover and disruptions in foster care are likely to enhance the attractiveness of residential homes, which appear better able than foster care provision to withstand the difficulties with which adolescents present (Rowe, Hundleby and Garnett 1989). All these considerations suggest a need to tackle the difficulties that have led to the decline in residential care, as distinct from looking forward to its demise.

The general landscape from within which residential child care policy and practice is delivered has changed considerably during the course of the past two decades. Along with major contemporary shifts in the size of homes, there have been changes in their purpose and function, in the ways services are organised and delivered, and in accountability, standards, registration and inspection (Barter et al. 2004; Mainey and Crimmens 2006). Additionally, awareness of the experiences and situations of those being looked after has been growing, with many major reforms occurring during the course of the last ten years, from *People Like Us: Report of the Review of Safeguards for Children Living Away from Home* (Utting 1997) through to the wide-ranging government Green Paper *Care Matters: Transforming the Lives of Children and Young People in Care* (Department for Education and Skills 2006a).[1] Other major initiatives include the Department of Health 'Quality Protects' and 'Choice Protects' programmes, which respectively focus on the management and delivery of children's social services and outcomes for looked after children. Further to these, the Children Act 2004 and the subsequent framework proposals advanced in *Every Child Matters: Change for Children* (Department for Education and Skills 2003) denote a distinct government emphasis on outcomes for children. These reforms, together with contextual shifts in the focus of policy concerning the overall well-being of children and young people, reflect a growing awareness of the need for, and national commitment towards, improvements in the life chances of young people living in residential care.

Throughout structural and policy shifts, variation in the actual performance of children's homes has remained an abiding and somewhat problematic feature. What accounts for the differences in what children's homes are able to achieve? How might 'promising practice' be supported better? The research on which this book is based took variation in performance as its central concern and sought to explain it. Our aims were to determine what it was that effective managers did, how this related to resources, and how what was done achieved a reasonable environment in the home or longer-term change in the resident young people.

Background

On 31 March 1978 there were approximately 31,000 children living in community homes in England and 33,000 living in foster care. In 2006 there were 42,000 children living in foster care but the numbers living in homes and hostels subject to Children's Homes regulations (under the April 2000 new coding structure) had shrunk to 6600 (Department for Education and Skills 2006b). The term 'children' in relation to residential care is somewhat misleading as the majority of residents at any one time are teenagers, with many experiencing fairly short placements. The decline of residential care overall, however, reflects a number of historical and well-documented difficulties.

One reason for the decline relates to values. Residential care was held in high esteem at a time when emphasis was placed on the group as opposed to the family or individual. Boarding schools in Russia, Israeli kibbutzim and public schools in England all, in different ways, reflected these values. By contrast, current social work gives a very high value to maintaining children in their own homes, or, if this fails, providing them with alternative 'family style' care (Department of Health 1989). Shifts in value provide a backdrop to the care of children. There remain a number of more specific difficulties for residential care. These provide the focus for our research.

The first problem is expense. A decade ago, residential care for children was shown to cost an estimated £61,000 per place per year (Carr-Hill *et al.* 1997). The Chartered Institute of Public Finance and Accountancy (CIPFA) figures relevant to the time period during which our research was conducted suggested a total of more than £735 million in England alone (CIPFA 2002). The total expenditure is more than that on foster care, which takes five times the number of children at any one time, and considerably more than the total spent by social services on children who are disabled or at risk (Carr-Hill *et al.* 1997).

A second problem concerns scandal and abuse. Major policy changes have aimed to reduce the frequency with which staff abuse children (for example, Kirkwood 1993; Levy and Kahan 1991; Utting 1991, 1997). Less attention has been paid to the harm that children may do to each other. One important study found that half the residents complained of attempted bullying or sexual harassment. Four out of ten said that they had considered killing themselves in the previous month. A measure of 'misery' was more strongly associated with experience of bullying or harassment in the home than it was with previous experiences (Sinclair and Gibbs 1998a). Another study found that the combination of conflictual characteristics relating to peer violence, although found individually in other settings, was unique in its concentration in children's homes (Barter *et al.* 2004).

A third, but related, problem concerns disorder. In the Sinclair and Gibbs (1998a) study, residents also complained of 'being led astray'. Statistics supported their concerns. Three-quarters of those with a previous conviction acquired a further caution or conviction if they stayed in the home for six months. Four out of ten of those who had no previous convictions or cautions and stayed this long were in trouble with the police. The great majority of those who stayed for any length of time ran away at least once (Sinclair and Gibbs 1998a). Evidence in that study suggested that delinquency in a home was strongly associated with bullying. It is probable that both factors provide a context within which sexual abuse is easier to conceal (Utting 1997).

A fourth problem concerns lack of effectiveness. There is considerable evidence that delinquency in particular is highly influenced by the immediate environment in which it occurs. Homes are able to have a considerable influence on the delinquent behaviour of residents while they are resident. The effect, however, is short-lived and the likelihood of further trouble is crucially dependent on the environment to which the resident returns (Allerhand, Weber and Haug 1966; Coates, Miller and Ohlin 1978; Sinclair 1971 and 1975; Taylor and Alpert 1973). Perhaps unsurprisingly, studies carried out when residential child care was at its peak generally failed to show that it had any long-term effect on delinquency (Brody 1976; Lipton, Martinson and Wilks 1975; Martinson 1974).

It was against this background that the residential child care research initiative was commissioned by the Department of Health (Department of Health 1998). This emphasised the variation in residential care, which in turn suggested a promising approach to its difficulties. In relation to costs, the research initiative found a great diversity in the resources available to homes. In one study (Sinclair and Gibbs 1998a) staff hours, which some have estimated as accounting for 80 per cent of the costs (Utting 1991), varied from 23 hours per place to 144. Much of this latter variation seemed related to local authority practice where CIPFA (2002) figures suggested that one authority may estimate an annual cost for a residential child care place three to four times as great as that estimated by another authority. So the question arose of whether this variation was matched by similar variations in the environment of the homes and the impact on residents in the longer term.

In relation to disorder, studies in the initiative and prior to that (Berridge and Brodie 1998; Sinclair and Gibbs 1998a; Tizard 1975) found wide differences in the behaviour of apparently similar young people living in different homes. Sinclair and Gibbs (1998a) found a striking concordance between the amount of delinquent behaviour among the young people as measured by running away and police contacts, the morale of the staff and the degree to which the staff and residents described the home as a reasonable place to live. Some homes seemed to be benign, others quite the reverse, and these differences apparently were not explained by differences in the backgrounds of those admitted. The existence of this diversity suggests that, if all homes functioned as well as the best, the residential environment could be considerably improved.

In combination (Berridge and Brodie 1998; Brown *et al.* 1998; Sinclair and Gibbs 1998a; Whitaker, Archer and Hicks 1998), the studies suggested that the variable performance of homes could be explained by three or possibly four factors. These included the leadership exercised by the manager of the home, the context within which the manager worked (notably the existence of clear, feasible goals for the home, which were agreed with senior management), a staff group unified behind their manager and, in one study, size and the degree to which the manager was able to articulate a clear philosophy.

The studies did not spell out exactly what it was that managers did, the relationship of this to resources, or how this related to the experiences of the young people. These questions form the core issues for the research described in this book; in addressing these questions, we built on hypotheses from previous work.

The practice of effective managers of children's homes

The studies cited earlier provided consistent insight into what the manager of the home needed to achieve. A key aim was to maintain a 'healthy' staff group that worked in secure and confident ways (Brown *et al.* 1998; Sinclair and Gibbs 1998a; Whitaker *et al.* 1998). In order to do this, managers had to concentrate on three objectives. First, they needed to ensure that staff had, or had access to, the necessary skills and knowledge base relevant to the work (Hicks, Archer and Whitaker 1998). Second, they needed to create and sustain a framework for practice – to establish the way that things were done in a particular home – that was agreed between themselves and their staff, among staff members themselves, and between staff and their external managers (Brown *et al.* 1998; Sinclair and Gibbs 1998a; Whitaker *et al.* 1998). Third, they needed both to ensure, and to bring about a sense, that resources were adequate to the tasks being performed (Whitaker *et al.* 1998).

In achieving these ends, important issues were the work that was done with managers external to the home (for detailed work on this area, see Whipp, Kirkpatrick and Kitchener 2005) and the 'boundaries' that were placed around the home itself. Managers of homes who were not in agreement with line managers (Brown *et al.* 1998), or who felt they did not have adequate autonomy to work within an agreed framework (Sinclair and Gibbs 1998a), seemed to find it harder to run effective homes, possibly because they lacked the authority to exercise effective leadership. Similarly, when the staff group was new or uncertain, a 'stronger' boundary was needed in order to enable a sense of home identity. When the staff group was more secure, greater permeability was possible and helped to ensure that the group remained open to new ideas and that poor practice did not become institutionalised. A suitably permeable boundary was one where staff members worked effectively from a secure base and operated competently with those external to the home. A boundary that was too permeable might result in external influences holding sway and staff being insecure; a boundary that was too tight might well encourage collusive practices (Whitaker *et al.* 1998).

One study (Whitaker *et al.* 1998) suggested that effective leadership also depended on the degree to which the manager of the home was a member of the staff group – more specifically, the degree to which she or he participated alongside their staff as a 'hands-on' staff-member, collaborated with staff in bringing about the framework within which work took place; held the authority of their position; and was prepared to act as a 'person of last resort'. The hypothesis was that effective practice for managers of children's homes required a balancing act. What seemed to be essential was that managers were able to occupy a position that was sufficiently 'hands-on' to enable them to model ways of working and to embody the ethos they wished to create and sustain. At the same time, managers had to be able to step away from working alongside staff members in such a way that they were able to show personal strength, security and leadership.

The style of the manager almost certainly had to be married to a secure sense of practice. Sinclair and Gibbs (1998a) interviewed managers about the ways in which they sought to achieve certain ends in the home (maintenance of resident health, the reduction of behavioural and emotional problems, and other dimensions involved in the looking after children initiative (see Parker *et al.* 1991 and Ward 1995). They created a measure of the degree to which managers had thought through the means of achieving their ends in these areas, and found that it related to changes in 'state' of the young people, as independently assessed by social workers.

These studies thus provided strong leads on the dimensions along which the work of managers should be explored and on the type of practice that was characteristic of effective managers. These leads, however, emerged within a range of other findings in studies that were not specifically concerned with the role of managers themselves. Moreover, they often expressed their conclusions in quite abstract terms such as 'leadership' or 'a framework for practice'. There arose a need both to refine and test these leads, and to formulate them to guide practice on the ground.

Use of resources in children's homes

Perhaps somewhat unfortunately, the studies suggested that the levers on which local authorities have relied implicitly to improve performance are not, in themselves, effective. A major concern was to improve the staffing ratios in homes and the proportion of qualified staff. These twin concerns have led to an explosion of costs. Only one study (Sinclair and Gibbs 1998a) looked statistically at the relationship between staffing ratios, the qualifications of staff and manager on the one hand and measures of the apparent effectiveness of the home on the other. The results were in keeping with a study associated with the initiative (Berridge and Brodie 1998), and were highly disappointing. In short, they found no relationship between these variables and the 'output' of homes. Strikingly, there was no association between a measure of the turbulence of homes and the number of staff hours available to them, the proportion of qualified staff, or the presence of a manager of the home. By contrast, there was some evidence that in any given size of home the greater the number of staff, the greater the degree of disorder, and that a high proportion of qualified staff was associated with low morale.

Overall, the negative findings on the effects of resources ran counter to the policy assumptions of around 50 years. They were contrary to the beliefs of staff. It was not possible to discern how or why some homes managed with fewer staff than others. Partly no doubt for these reasons, the conclusions drawn (at that point these had been reported upon although remained unpublished) were rightly treated by the Utting report (1997) with very considerable caution. On the face of it, however, they were important. They urgently needed testing and their practice implications needed to be understood.

Aims of the research

It was clear that research stemming from these studies needed to articulate its hypotheses, test them and look at the implications for practice. This is the task we set ourselves with the project on which this book is based. As noted earlier, we aimed to describe the practice of managers of children's homes, the ways they used the resources at their disposal, and their attendant costs. We set out to assess the impact of these variables on the morale and unity of the staff group, on the quality of the residential environment, and on changes in the residents during the course of a single year. We also wanted to assess our conclusions against their applicability to practice, and the experience of staff and their managers. In these ways, we set out to develop an understanding of the key issues of costs, the residential environment and longer-term effectiveness.

Our research was one of 13 studies funded by the Department of Health under the 'Costs and Effectiveness of Services to Children in Need' research initiative. The initiative was concerned to examine the way 'services were delivered, the costs of providing services and the extent to which they improve outcomes for children in contact with social care services' (Beecham and Sinclair 2007, p.13). Our research was necessarily multi-disciplinary and the involvement of an economic component provided an exciting opportunity to develop social care research.

Research methods and ethics

The project involved a quantitative study of 45 homes (30 local authority and 15 independent sector homes), a qualitative study of homes managers' roles, and a further qualitative study of a sub-sample of ten homes selected to present contrasts in resource use and leadership styles and characteristics. Appropriate ethical conduct was observed throughout the project and its dissemination.[2] The homes and young people living in them were described at two points in time, approximately a year apart. Information about the young people and the homes at these two points was related to variations in costs, size, the approach of the manager of the home and other factors likely to affect performance. The overall aim was to test the hypotheses outlined earlier through statistical techniques, through the analysis of concrete examples of practice, and through direct discussion of the conclusions with managers of homes and their staff groups.

Descriptions of the methods in each component of the project are given in the respective chapters of the book and a comprehensive overview of the methods used is provided in Appendix A, 'Research Methodology'.

Structure of the book

Having outlined the context and background to the research we carried out and its aims and methods, the book reports in detail what we found. In subsequent chapters, we provide overviews from the various data sources – namely, the survey data, the qualitative data and the economics data. A key feature of the book will be seen to be that of diversity, in those living and working in children's homes, in the way that children's homes are managed and led, and in the ways in which resources are used and their attendant costs. In the penultimate chapter, we consider the impact of these differences. This allows us to tackle the central question of the research – namely, how far do the outcomes of children's homes depend on the characteristics of residents, the resources expended, or the practice of the staff and managers?

Following from this first, introductory, chapter, we provide in Chapter 2 a description of the children's homes in our sample, as drawn from survey information that focused on the participating children's homes themselves, the young people living in the homes and views from their field social workers, and the staff working in our sample of homes. In Chapters 3, 4 and 5, we focus on describing the roles of the managers of children's homes. We draw on qualitative data obtained through interviews with managers of homes, group discussions with managers and staff, and written responses from questionnaire data. From the qualitative material, we formulate in Chapter 6 a conceptualisation of leadership in children's homes. Our final descriptive strand is drawn together in Chapter 7, which entails economic data, including information from and about homes themselves in terms of the way they use resources and other services, and data from the homes' attendant finance offices and departments. Having summarised our data, in Chapter 8 we move on to drawing out where differences lie, and explaining these by turning to an analysis of the variations we have identified in terms of what differences these make to outcomes for young people. We close by summarising in Chapter 9 the main findings from each part of the project and look at their implications for practice, policy and training.

A note about vocabulary: we started out by referring to 'heads' of homes. During the course of the project we adopted the now more widely accepted term 'manager' or 'residential manager'. This role is not to be confused with that of the line manager to the home, which is identified throughout as the 'external manager' or 'line manager'. Additionally, as noted earlier, the term 'children's home' is of course somewhat misleading. The majority of young people who live in 'children's homes' are over ten years old and throughout this book we mainly use the term 'young people' to refer to residents. In practice settings, the term 'young people' is used most frequently to refer to those living in children's homes; however, the terms 'children', 'adolescents', 'teenagers', 'young people' and at times 'young adults' are also in common usage.

The approach taken in each part of the research determines the way it is reported; there are several perspectives in use overall and our analysis builds incrementally on the discrete methodological strands. By their nature, the chapters of the book vary in the way they present material, with some being more technically oriented than others. Necessarily, there is something of a gear shift between different sections of the book as they spring from different approaches. In the three statistically informed chapters – 2, 7 and 8 – we provide narratives in addition to tables to assist in understanding the points being made. The end of each chapter includes a summary of key points. We are mindful that the majority of readers may not share in enthusiasm for the detail of particular statistical techniques that integrate the various dimensions of the project; for those readers who do, we have provided Appendix B, 'Sample Models'.

Summary

Residential child care in England and Wales occupies an important position in the continuum of services provided for children and young people looked after away from home. Over the years, children's homes have been faced with considerable challenges, where problems of expense, scandal and abuse, disorder and lack of effectiveness have been well documented. These have prompted major initiatives designed to raise and monitor standards, and improve the structure and functioning of the system overall. The general decline in the number of homes, the high turnover of residents, prevailing complex levels of need, and increases in costs have resulted in children's homes continuing to experience difficulties in establishing consistent and coherent cultures. This chapter has given a brief overview of the background, aims and methods of the research on which the book is based.

The research reported here aimed to identify the ways in which effective homes managers work, how this relates to resources, and how this links to achieving a reasonable environment in the home, or longer-term change in the residents. We move on to show how our aims were realised.

We turn now to Chapter 2, where we look at material from the surveys carried out during the course of our research.

Notes

1   Other notable influences include *Me, Survive Out There? New Arrangements for Young People Living in and Leaving Care* (Department of Health 1999); the Children (Leaving Care) Act 2000; the Care Standards Act 2000; the Adoption and Children Act 2002; and *A Better Education for Children in Care* (Social Exclusion Unit 2003).

2   Awareness of ethical conduct and governance in relation to social science research has increased rapidly during recent years and is a matter for keen contemporary debate. However, to date there does not exist a national system of ethical approval for social care research. The research on which this book is based was conducted according to the Social Research Association's *Ethical Guidelines*, first published in the 1980s and regularly revised, with the most recent version being published in 2003 (Social Research Association [SRA] 2003). Since the research reported here was commissioned, many University Social Science Ethics Committees have been established, which provide formal opportunities for ethical scrutiny of each project as it becomes funded. As the SRA acknowledges in its *Guidelines*, responsibility for ethical conduct is held ultimately by researchers and their funding bodies. The team involved in this research was committed to good practice throughout the course of the project. As will be seen, the complex nature of the project required close attention to hierarchical permissions routes, informed consent, confidentiality, ways of enabling participation and protecting the interests of those taking part. Clearly these areas are all within the bounds of good ethical conduct and do not demand special credit, although we do consider them to be worthy of discrete note here.

Chapter 2

Who Lives and Works in Children's Homes?

Introduction

The chapters of this book contribute towards an integrated understanding of what needs to be taken into account when establishing and maintaining good practice for and on behalf of young people living in children's homes. In so doing, the book examines the functional relationships of structure, process and outcome within residential child care. For example, we investigate whether or not the structural characteristics of the home influence, positively or negatively, the process of care and whether changes in the process of care, including variations in its amount and quality – both aspects of how resources are managed – will influence the effect that care has on the physical, social and psychological well-being of young people.

The links between structure, process and outcome form part of an established body of literature about organisational performance, based on the work of Avedis Donabedian. Donabedian (1966, 1980, 1982, 1988, 1993) offers 'structure', 'process' and 'outcome' (SPO) as the three main approaches for examining care in different settings. 'Structure' represents the relative stable characteristics of the providers of care, the resources they have at their disposal, and the physical and organisational settings in which they work. Whereas such variables as the age of the building and the staff to resident ratio may vary between different providers, to a large extent they are constants within residential homes. The 'process' of care, on the other hand, is the set of activities that take place within and between those who provide care and those who receive it. In the context of the study described in this book, an 'outcome' denotes those aspects of a young person's well-being that can be linked to the care provided. As such, it includes social and psychological functioning as well as the physical condition of the young person.

Later chapters in this book deal extensively with 'process' and 'outcomes'. In the present chapter, however, we focus on aspects of 'structure', including a depiction of those living and working in children's homes. The chapter summarises the extensive survey data that were collected over the two main points of data collection: Time 1 (T1) and, 10–12 months later, Time 2 (T2). In doing so it fulfils three main functions by providing:

1. context – in describing the homes (the buildings from which they operate, the staff and children who work and live in them, and the outcomes) the chapter provides the necessary background for locating the rest of the study

2. comparison – at various points the chapter sets out the results from the present study alongside those from earlier studies in order to draw out features that have remained relatively constant or similar, and those where this is not the case

3. identification of the main sources of variation between homes – as preparation for a later chapter that assesses whether, after making due allowance for the key differences between homes, these characteristics or inputs influence outcomes.

It should be noted that the chapter is organised around the main survey instruments employed in this part of the study. By way of introduction, Table 2.1 sets out a summary of the instruments used, along with the final response rates.

As can be seen, we sent a separate questionnaire at T2 to 118 young people who had moved on from their original T1 home to a new destination. We received 48 replies. Tracking the whereabouts of this group was problematic and part of the non-response should be viewed more accurately as non-contact. While the numbers are small, and the ability to make generalisations limited, it was interesting to note that over one-third (35%) of the young people had in fact transferred to another children's home, just under a quarter (23%) had gone to birth parents or relatives and just over a quarter (27%) were living independently. Few, however, had been found a suitable foster placement.

Given the constraints on space, it is not possible to present and discuss every single finding yielded by the 14 surveys. Instead, we concentrate on the broad themes that emerge from the surveys at T1 and T2. To aid this task, we have organised the rest of this section into five parts, the first four corresponding to the main sources of data set out in Table 2.1, and a fifth that draws together some of the key areas of diversity.

Table 2.1 The instruments used in the main surveys and response rates

		T1	T2
1a	*Details of Home – Basic Information*	sent=45: returned=41	sent=40: returned=28
1b	*Details of Home – Current Staff Log*	information provided on 486 current staff in 41 homes	information provided on 314 current staff
1c	*Details of Home – Current Resident Log*	information provided on 206 current residents in 41 homes	information provided on 132 current residents
1d	*Details of Home – Past Resident Log*	information provided on 217 past residents in 35 homes	information provided on 125 past residents
2	*Staff Questionnaire*	sent=550: returned=301 (55%)	*Not administered at T2*
3a	*Young Person's Questionnaire – Living in Children's Home* (YPQ1)	sent=226: returned=175 (77%)	T1 YPs still in home at T2 sent=92: returned=70 (76%) 'New' YPs in home at T2 sent=95: returned=72 (76%)
3b	*Young Person's Questionnaire – No Longer Living in Children's Home* (YPQ2)	Not administered at T1	sent=118: returned=48 (41%)
4	*Social Worker Questionnaire (SWQ)*	sent=226: returned=134 (60%)	sent=187: returned=103 (55%)

1. The homes: staff, current and past residents
The homes

In total, the study contained 45 homes, 41 of which returned the *Details of Home Questionnaire* at T1. From Table 2.1 it can be seen that this questionnaire contained sections that covered basic information about the homes (1a), the staff who worked in them (1b), the young people who were currently living in the homes (1c) and those young people who had done so over the last 12 months (1d).

Half the homes in the present study had opened during the decade 1991–2001, and the other half before this decade, the oldest in 1926. The age of the building in which the homes operated ranged from mid-Victorian villas to recent, purpose-built houses. On balance, homes in the independent sector tended to occupy the older premises.

A major change over the last decade has been the general move away from large, multi-bedded homes to those of a smaller size. This trend was reflected in this study where none of the homes contained more than ten beds. Indeed, nearly three-quarters (73%) contained seven beds or fewer, with one home intended to care for just one young person.

Just over a quarter of the homes (11 out of 41, or 27%) had experienced a major change of function over the last 12 months. This change involved four out of five homes in one authority, both homes in another, and the remaining five spread throughout the rest of the providers. Examples of change included the extending of the age range, a pilot scheme for an 'all boys' home to be reviewed after a year, and a change of focus to working with birth families and preparing young people for fostering.

From the answers given to the final question in this part of the question-naire, nine out of ten homes routinely recorded the information we required for that part of the project that dealt with costs and the use of services by young people in the home.

The staff

For many years very little was known about residential staff in general or those in children's homes in particular. However, considerable knowledge and understanding about the characteristics and role of staff in children's homes was provided in the late 1990s through our previous work (Sinclair and Gibbs 1998a; Whitaker *et al.* 1998). Apart from the importance of staff in the role they play in influencing outcomes, it is well established in studies of health and social care that staff costs account for a substantial proportion of overall costs. For this reason it is important to know how many staff, or more precisely how many staff hours, are available. With this information, along with the number of children in the home, it was possible to replicate a measure that Sinclair and Gibbs (1998a) had used in an earlier study to explore the variation in the number of care hours available to each child.

The *Current Staff Log* provided basic biographical details on each member of staff in the home at that stage, including their age, sex, post, length of time in post and qualifications. We are able to compare the results for several of these items with the same items in the *Staff Questionnaire* to determine the representativeness of the returns. Table 2.2 sets out the results; the columns on the left give the results for the T1 data collection in 2001.

Table 2.2 Characteristics of staff in *Staff Log* and *Staff Questionnaire* returns

	Staff Log (n=486) %	Staff Questionnaire (n=301) %
Sex		
Males	34.6	33.9
Females	65.4	66.1
Age		
Under 30	17.6	15.7
30–39	33.3	34.1
40–49	28.2	28.3
50 and over	20.9	21.8
Mean (age)	*39.8*	*39.9*
Main qualification		
DipSW/CQSW/CSS	11.1	*Question not asked*
Cert C Care/Nursery N	7.0	
Teacher Training	0.6	
NVQ+Other (unspecified)	27.9	
None	53.3	
Hours		
Under 20	6.9	5.0
20–29	7.9	9.4
30–38	62.8	60.0
39 and over	22.4	25.6
Mean (hours)	*35.0*	*35.5*

Continued on next page

Table 2.2 continued

	Staff Log (n=486) %	Staff Questionnaire (n=301) %
Time in home		
Less than 2 years	41.8	31.2
2 years, under 3 years	10.5	14.3
3–4 years	15.0	21.3
5 years and over	32.9	33.2
Mean (years)	*4.6*	*4.4*
Post		
Manager/Supervisor	28.6	22.6
Care staff	59.0	67.8
Domestic and other staff	12.4	9.6
Ethnicity		
White British/White Other	94.0	*Question not asked*
African-Caribbean	4.1	
Asian	0.4	
Mixed Afro-Caribb: White	1.0	
Mixed Asian: White	0.4	

Sources: *Staff Log* data and *Staff Questionnaire* data.

In all important respects, the data for the 2001 questionnaire and staff respondents were sufficiently similar for us to proceed with confidence that those who returned the *Staff Questionnaire* in the current study were representative of the whole staff group. A little later we will outline the views expressed in the latter questionnaire, but for the moment we consider the characteristics of the staff who worked in the homes as recorded in the *Current Staff Log*.

Similar to the earlier study, the ratio of female to male staff in the present study was about two to one. Few staff of either sex were drawn from minority ethnic groups despite major conurbations (including a London borough) participating in the project. There was no evidence to suggest that men were more likely than women to be in senior posts, although it was clear that significantly more women (23%) than men (6%) worked part-time. Overall, the majority of staff (83%) worked full-time on permanent contracts. Homes in the present study tended to have fewer 'domestic and other staff' than previously. Both the *Log* and the *Staff Questionnaire* yielded very similar results for the number of contracted hours worked by different categories of staff – on average, managers and deputies worked 37.4 hours per week, care staff 35.5 and domestic and other staff 28.6 hours per week. Two-thirds of the managers and deputies, one-third of the care staff and about one in ten domestic and other staff were also working overtime each week (on average just over 12 hours a week for managers, 11.5 hours for care staff and other staff).

The homes are characterised by a large number of staff who have been in post for less than two years matched by an equally large proportion, especially senior staff, who have been in post for five years or more. Taking a wider perspective, two-thirds (66%) of staff have at least five years' experience of working in residential care generally. Senior care staff are more likely to possess a Diploma in Social Work (DipSW)/Certificate of Qualification in Social Work (CQSW) or Certificate in Social Service (CSS), and far less likely to have no qualifications than other care staff; most staff are employed on contracts, and one in six had been promoted over the last year.

This then is a general overview of the staff who work in the homes. However, considerable differences emerge when the overall results are broken down in different ways. We take three examples to illustrate the general point about variation in the overall result.

First, there are differences between homes, between providers and between sectors in the age of staff – the sector analysis indicates that the average age of staff is 41.2 and 34.8 years in local authority and independent homes, respectively.

Second, in terms of qualifications held by staff, the three independent variables show significant differences. The sector analysis for this item indicates that whereas proportionally more local authority staff possess a CQSW or equivalent qualification, or no qualification at all, than their colleagues in the independent sector, proportionally more of the latter have gained a National Vocational Qualification (NVQ) or its equivalent.

Third, there were very varying perceptions of the adequacy of staffing. Under-staffing was reported as a problem by the managers of 35 out of the 41 homes, with 13 (32%) indicating that this was a 'severe' problem. The differences were very much between organisations/providers rather than at sector level. To illustrate this point, whereas all four homes of one of the independent providers reported separately that under-staffing was not a problem, three out of five homes of another independent provider reported severe problems. Similarly, some local authority providers experienced more perceived problems than others.

The main point we wish to emphasise is that considerable variation occurs when the overall characteristics of staff, as recorded in the *Staff Log*, are looked at more closely. This can be related to a variety of outcome measures. To give an example, overall, staff sickness emerged as a major factor associated with under-staffing as reported by the managers in the *Details of Home Questionnaire*. With data available from a variety of sources, it was possible to see how the question of staff sickness related to other variables – for example, to the perceptions of staff themselves. Linking staff sickness as a reason for under-staffing to information in the T1 *Staff Questionnaire* indicates that it is associated with a measure of general concerns expressed by staff, whether they themselves thought there was sufficient staff to run the home and with their own satisfaction with the leadership in the home. Of course, associations of this type do not necessarily imply causal relationships; although variables such as size are fixed, others vary and are perhaps better seen as outcomes.

Current residents

We turn now to the characteristics of the young people living in the homes at T1. Table 2.1 indicates that basic information, ranging from their age to the amount of time they had lived in the home, was provided on 206 young people in the *Current Resident Log*.

While we recruited to the study homes that were both non-specialist and broadly comparable in purpose and function, it is to be expected that on some items differences will exist. Some, as we have seen, were single-sex homes, whereas others specialised in preparing young people for independence. Given this explanation, it is not surprising that the young people differed according to the function and purpose of the home. The results display significant differences when looked at in terms of the three main independent variables. We will not dwell on every result but will take two to illustrate the general point about variation between homes, providers and sectors.

The first concerns 'exclusion' from school. While, according to Brodie (2001), the term lacks precision, the reality is that if young people do not go to school their education is disrupted and their future prospects yet further constrained. In addition, absence from school often involves young people hanging around the home getting in the way of staff or, left to their own devices, getting into mischief outside the home. In the present study, whereas proportionally more young people living in independent homes than in local authority homes had been excluded from school before entry to the home, the reverse held when it came to school exclusion during their time in the home.

The most probable explanation for this finding is the greater number of independent homes with education on the premises.

A second difference concerns the average number of days young people have spent in their homes. Like so many of the results, there are differences between homes and between providers but not, at first glance at least, between sectors. The average (as measured by the mean) was just under one year in both sectors (local authority: 350 days, independent: 360 days). However, taking the median (the middle value of the range), rather than the mean average, gives 236 days and 320 days, respectively. In other words, local authority homes take some long-staying residents but also a higher proportion of short-stay ones than do homes in the independent sector.

Before outlining the corresponding results for the young people who had left the home over the last 12 months ('past residents'), Table 2.3 provides a summary of the results from the *Current Resident Log* and the *Past Resident Log*.

Past residents

These are the 217 young people, other than the 206 current residents, who had lived in the home over the last 12 months. Given that one local authority home and five independent sector homes had no young people who had left over this period, the analysis concerns 35 of the 41 homes that returned the questionnaire. Again, we asked for the same range of information as for the current residents.

The young people ranged in age from infants aged 2 to young adults aged 19, with the largest proportion (43%) aged 14 or 15. The age of young people differed by the three main independent variables – homes, organisation and sector. All the very young children aged 6 years or under (n=5) were living in local authority homes as were 51 of the 53 young people aged 16 and over.

The proportion of males to females (about 60:40) did not vary by the three main independent variables. However, five items ('ethnic background', 'legal status', 'school exclusion', 'going missing', 'convictions') all varied by 'home' and 'organisation'. In general terms, for example, there were some homes with significantly more young people from minority ethnic groups than other homes, even within the same local authority or organisation. The same was true at the level of organisation – that is, some local authorities or independent providers had proportionally more young people from minority ethnic groups than others.

It can be seen from Table 2.3 that the two measures of central tendency that we give – the mean (209 days) and the median (62 days) – differ

Table 2.3 Summary of results from *Current* and *Past Resident Logs*

		Current Resident Log (n=206) %	Past Resident Log (n=217) %
Sex	Males	58.3	62.2
	Females	41.7	37.8
Age	11 years and under	13.1	13.4
	12/13 years	18.9	18.4
	14/15 years	48.1	42.9
	16 years and over	19.9	25.3
Ethnicity	White	91.3	94.9
	Other	8.7	5.1
Legal status	Looked after	51.9	63.6
	Subject to order	48.1	31.8
	Remanded to care	–	4.6
Excluded from school before entry to home	Yes	35.4	48.0
	No	64.6	52.0
Excluded from school during time in home	Yes	22.3	23.3
	No	77.7	76.7
Run away/Gone missing[1]	No(ne)	50.5	50.3
	1–5 times	29.6	34.6
	6 or more times	19.9	15.1
Convicted before entry to home	Yes	33.3	36.3
	No	66.7	63.7
Convicted during time in home	Yes	28.5	22.6
	No	71.5	77.4
Time in home	In days	Mean=352	Mean=209
		Median=269	Median=62
	1 month or less	5.0	41.0
	1 month to 1 year	58.5	39.2
	More than a year	36.5	19.8

Sources: *Current* and *Past Resident Log* data.

Note: 1 Defined as running away from children's home or unauthorised absence overnight.

considerably. This reflects a wide array of stays from one day to 2802 days (7.6 years) with many young people (41%) staying for a month or less and a smaller (20%), but significant, group staying for a year or more. Although the details are not shown in the table, this variable also varied by home, organisation and sector. The sector analysis revealed, for example, that past residents stayed 292 days on average in independent sector homes compared to 191 days in local authority sector homes.

2. The views and experience of staff working in homes

Our justification for seeking the views of staff was that, while the philosophy and routines of the home may be determined largely by the organisation and manager, it is the staff who have to implement these and whose day-to-day actions help establish the 'climate' in the home. We achieved a 60 per cent response to the *Staff Questionnaire*, similar to the staff response (58%) in our earlier study (Sinclair and Gibbs 1998a). Given that we have covered the basic characteristics of staff earlier (in our discussion of the *Staff Log*), we now turn our attention to whether their views and experience differed according to the range of independent variables included in the analysis.

An early section of the *Staff Questionnaire* asked a range of questions about the preparation and training staff had received, including the first of two questions about overall satisfaction with the job. The analyses for the 14 individual items in this section indicate that, apart from three exceptions when 'post' was considered, there were no significant differences when we looked at the items in terms of the independent variables related to the respondent ('age', 'sex' and 'post'). On the other hand, consistent differences emerged for the analyses involving 'home', 'organisation' and 'sector'. Closer inspection of the results indicates that any 'dissatisfaction' on an item tends to be clustered in one or two homes within an authority, which gives rise to the differences in the homes' analysis, and this, in turn, is reflected in the analysis for organisation and sector.

A separate question about satisfaction with training brought about a similar result (an overall high level of satisfaction (eight in ten members of staff were at least 'satisfied' with the training they had received) with significant variation on the group independent variables.

On the basis of a list of concerns that staff in children's homes had raised about their jobs, we asked staff in this study to rate the items in terms of the concern they had caused them. Overall, the two items that caused the greatest concern were the residents' progress and the money for the job; conversely, relations with other staff and with young people were items where at least two-thirds of staff indicated 'no concern'.

Our earlier work (Sinclair and Gibbs 1998a) had shown that 'social climate' (i.e. the way that staff, young people and, to a lesser extent, families, are treated and behave towards one another) was an important explanation for the variations between homes. For this reason we included the same items in the *Staff Questionnaire* as had been used before and included fresh items that tapped aspects of leadership and staff relationships in the home. We employed a series of simple statements – for example, 'This home is a friendly place' as a way of measuring 'social climate'. Further analysis indicated that it was possible to combine many (but not all) of the items to create the following sub-scales:

- Scale 1 – staff views on whether home friendly place (5 items)
- Scale 2 – staff views on behaviour of young people (3 items)
- Scale 3 – staff views on commitment of young people to home (2 items)
- Scale 4 – staff views on leadership in home (4 items)
- Scale 5 – staff views on whether sufficient staff (4 items)
- Scale 6 – staff views on staff cohesion (3 items).

We found that, of the independent variables, 'home', 'organisation' and, to an extent, 'sector' displayed the greatest variation.

We complete this brief overview of results from the *Staff Questionnaire* with a consideration of staff morale that, from the perspective of several items in the questionnaire, was generally high. The association of staff morale, as measured by the item 'Overall satisfaction with the job', with other items is set out in Table 2.4 – the figure is the correlation coefficient (the higher the coefficient 'r', the greater the association) and asterisks indicate the level of statistical significance (all the associations are highly significant). Apart from the negative value (r=−.48) for the association between 'overall staff satisfaction' and 'staff concerns' (staff who have 'concerns' are less likely to be satisfied overall with their jobs), the rest are positive. So, for example, if staff are satisfied with the training they have received, they are also likely to be satisfied with their jobs overall (r=.42 denotes a close and significant association between the two).

In contrast to the findings of our previous research, we were unable to establish in the present study any significant association between staff morale and the amount of time staff had spent in residential work in general or in their current home in particular. Unsurprisingly, however, there were large and significant variations between homes in both staff morale and the variables associated with it.

Table 2.4 Association of various measures with staff satisfaction

Measure	Staff satisfaction r
Staff views on whether sufficient staff in home	.34***
Staff views on staff cohesion	.23***
Staff concern score	−.48***
Staff views on young person's view of behaviour in home	.24***
Staff views on leadership in home	.30***
Overall satisfaction with amount of training	.42***
Frequency of supervision	.28***

Source: *Staff Questionnaire* data.
Note: ***Statistically significant at the .001 level.

3. The views and experiences of young people

The T1 *Questionnaire to Young People* was returned by 175 young people (77% response rate). Their basic characteristics were very similar to those recorded in the *Current Resident Log* (see Table 2.3), an indication that they were representative of the whole group of young people in the homes.

Nine out of ten of the young people were, or should have been, attending school – about 10 per cent were excluded from school. School exclusion was confined largely to young people aged 14 and 15, and involved both boys and girls in equal proportion. Those excluded from school were also those who scored highest on the 'pressure to temptation' scale that we will return to a little later.

Most young people (64%+) got on very well with staff in the homes and were at least 'happy' with the range of routines, arrangements and activities that regulate and mediate the experience of living in a children's home. A notable exception was the behaviour of other residents where over a third of the young people (36%) expressed disquiet.

Similar to our attempt in the *Staff Questionnaire* to obtain a measure or measures of social climate in the home, we asked the young people to respond to many of the same simple statements (but not the ones to do with 'leadership'). Again most of the items, but not all, could be combined to form the following smaller number of sub-scales:

- Scale 1 – the views of young people on whether home friendly place (5 items)
- Scale 2 – the views of young people on behaviour of young people (3 items)
- Scale 3 – the views of young people on commitment of others to home (2 items)
- Scale 4 – the views of young people on their involvement in the home (4 items).

Similar to the results for the social climate sub-scales in the *Staff Questionnaire*, we found that, of the independent variables, 'home', 'organisation' and 'sector' displayed the greatest variation when it came to the four social climate sub-scales in the *Questionnaire to Young People*.

We then asked the young people questions based on the well-established *Lancashire Quality of Life Profile* (Oliver *et al.* 1997). One question asked them to mark on an image of a ladder (developed originally by Cantril 1965) how they felt life was at the moment (the higher up the ladder the better life was); a further question asked them to choose from a list of statements the one that best described how they felt about their life as a whole.

Table 2.5 sets out some of the results for the 'ladder' of how young people feel at the moment (the original scores, which ranged from 0 to 100, have been placed into one of four broad groups). Initial analysis of the 'ladder' scores would suggest that, on average, boys are happier with their life at the moment than girls, and that young people living in homes in the independent sector are happier on this measure than those living in local authority homes.

The relationship between how young people feel at the moment (as measured by the ladder) and how they feel about their life as a whole is summarised for the statistically minded in the correlation coefficient $r=.64$. In lay terms, this signifies a close association between the two – for example, young people who feel pleased with their life at the moment tend to feel pleased with their life as a whole. This is not true of course for every young person, as Table 2.6 demonstrates. Here it can be seen that 80 per cent of young people who scored very low on the ladder (25 or less) also indicated that they were not pleased with their life as a whole. Conversely, nearly 57 per cent of those who scored very high on the ladder (75 or above) were also pleased with their life as a whole. For others, however, there is a disparity between the two.

Table 2.5 Grouped 'ladder' scores by sex and sector

Grouped 'ladder' score	Males (n=98) %	Females (n=77) %	Local Auth. (n=129) %	Independent (n=46) %	Overall (n=175) %
0–25	13.3	22.1	20.9	6.5	17.1
26–50	16.3	27.3	26.4	6.5	21.1
51–75	32.7	29.9	27.1	43.5	31.4
76–100	37.8	20.8	25.6	43.5	30.3
Mean score	*60.17*	*50.62*	*51.06*	*69.72*	*55.97*
Median score	*59.00*	*51.00*	*51.00*	*68.00*	*58.00*

Source: T1 *Questionnaire to Young People.*

Table 2.6 Association between life at the moment and life as a whole

Ladder scores grouped	n	Life as a whole – redefined		
		Not pleased %	Mixed %	Pleased %
0–25	30	80.0	16.7	3.3
26–50	37	27.0	48.6	24.4
51–75	55	12.7	45.5	41.8
76–100	53	3.8	39.6	56.6
Total	175	24.6	39.4	36.0

Source: T1 *Questionnaire to Young People.*
Note: Percentages add up to 100 across the rows.

We then asked the young people to respond to a number of statements about their possible feelings and how they saw themselves – for example, 'I have felt that I'm getting somewhere in life.' Our analysis of the responses indicated that it was possible to summate the scores of the nine individual items to form a sub-scale that we called 'esteem' and used, along with other summary measures, in our subsequent analyses. The correlation between esteem and the ladder was .467 – not as large as the correlation between 'life at the moment'

(Q7) and 'life as a whole' (Q9) but, in statistical terms, significant nonetheless. It was also evident that boys and young men had significantly higher esteem scores than girls and young women – a finding in accord with similar measures such as the ladder scores.

On the question of whether the home had helped the young person, the response was a resounding 'yes' from nearly 8 out of 10 of the young people. We asked ourselves whether there was anything that particularly character-ised the young people who felt that this was not the case. While there were few clues in terms of the independent variables, we had more success when we looked at the association between this item and the ladder and esteem scores. In brief, the minority (22%) of young people who felt that the home had not helped them scored significantly lower on the ladder and esteem scores than those who felt positive about the effects of the home. Again, however, we are faced with the issue of circularity – was it their experience of the home that brought about their dissatisfaction with life at the moment and their poor self-esteem, or the other way round?

The last of the 'closed' questions asked the young people about various temptations and pressures they had been subjected to both during their time in the home and before they arrived. In some respects the experience of the young people, according to their accounts, was similar both in and outside the home – for example, encouragement to get drunk and the offer of cannabis declined only marginally once young people were living in the home. However, there was considerably less pressure to temptation for some other items, such as stealing, once the young people were living in the homes.

Bullying, both perceived and real, is a highly significant contemporary issue defined by Mellor (1990, p.1) as '"long-standing" violence, mental or physical, conducted by an individual or a group against an individual who is not able to defend himself or herself in the situation'. It is a feature of institutional life as Farmer and Pollock (1998) confirmed in their study of children and young people who had been involved with sexual abuse, either as active abusers or through being abused themselves. The children in their study were 'looked after' in varying settings and roughly half had either bullied others or had been bullied themselves. Bullying appeared to be a particularly serious problem in children's homes, where it often continued over a long period without detection.

Indeed, bullying remained a problem in the present study and reinforced a point that we have made elsewhere (Gibbs and Sinclair 2000) – namely, that the greatest threat to young people is far more likely to come from other young people in the home rather than from staff. About half (48%) the young people said they had been bullied before arrival and about four out of ten (41%) said they had been bullied after it. As can be seen in Table 2.7, there was some continuity to the extent that six out of ten who had been bullied before reported that this had continued during their time living in the home; conversely, eight out of ten of those who had not experienced bullying before their arrival confirmed that this was still the case while living in the home.

For some the situation changed, most notably for the four out of ten young people who had been bullied before but not after arrival. However, the absence of bullying for this group was not reflected in the main outcome measures ('Life now', 'Life as a whole', 'Whether the home has helped') that remained much the same regardless of whether the young person had been bullied or not before or after arrival in the home or a combination of the two.

Table 2.7 Bullying before and during time in home

Bullied before arrival	n	Bullied during time in home %	
		Yes	No
Yes	91	60.7	39.3
No	84	22.0	78.0
Total	175	59.4	40.6

Source: T1 *Questionnaire to Young People.*
Note: Percentages add up to 100 across the rows.

We sent the same questionnaire at T2 to all young people living at that time in homes that were still part of the study (n=40) and received 142 replies (70 from young people who had been in the same home at T1 and 72 from young people who had arrived after T1). We made a number of checks to see whether the homes were essentially perceived in the same way by the new arrivals in the home as by those who had responded to the original T1 questionnaire and found this, by and large, to be the case.

4. The views and information provided by field social workers

So far we have considered the homes, the staff who work in them and the young people who live in them. To understand the reasons why young people are placed in residential care, what the homes are supposed to do with them once they are there, and where they are supposed to go next, we turn to the accounts provided by social workers.

We sent 226 questionnaires to the social workers of the young people in the T1 sample and received 134 replies (a 60% response). While the replies were a very close match to the main sample in terms of the age and ethnic background of the young people, boys (at 63%) were slightly over-represented in the social worker replies (Table 2.3 indicates that 58.3% of current residents were boys).

According to their social workers, four out of ten of the young people had been living with a parent(s) before they came to their present children's home, just over a fifth (22%) had been living with foster carers and just over a quarter (26%) had moved from another children's home. On average these young people had been 'looked after' for 36.9 months, although this ranged from as little as 3 days to over 12 years. Boys had been 'looked after', on average, for 42 months compared to 28 months for girls.

The figures for family composition are striking and closely resemble those in our previous study. For example, 37.4 per cent and 15.8 per cent of young people, respectively, in the present study were from a single-parent family or were living with both birth parents compared to 36.9 per cent and 15.9 per cent in our earlier study. Only a quarter (24.9%) of the young people were from families involving their birth father and it is not too difficult to imagine the sadness, clash of loyalties and confusion for them over the break-up of their parents' relationships. Very few of the families were thought by social workers to be caring, accepting and encouraging of their children, and even fewer still were considered able to be clear in their expectations of their children or able to see things from their child's point of view. Social workers also thought that abuse (physical, sexual or emotional) was a major problem for nearly a third (32%) of the young people for whom they returned questionnaires.

Against this less than promising background, it is perhaps surprising that not more young people exhibited behavioural difficulties. Apart from small minorities who, before their arrival in the home, were engaged in persistent delinquency (16%) or such activities as sexual behaviour that posed a risk to the young person and/or to others (13%), the major problem was truancy and/or school exclusion (40% in the present study; 41% in our earlier study). Most of these problems, however, decreased notably during the time the young person lived in the children's home, including school exclusion.

The next section of the *Questionnaire to Social Workers* asked a number of questions adapted from the LAC (Looking After Children) categories (see Parker *et al.* 1991; Ward 1995) that assess different aspects of a young person's development. While it was encouraging to learn from social workers that very few of the young people suffered ill health or failed to thrive, it is a cause for concern that so many of them were rated low on most of the other categories – for example, just over half (51%) were rated 'low', and a further fifth (19%) 'very low', on self-confidence. In spite of this, social workers remained fairly positive in their judgement about the overall progress of six out of ten of the young people (rated 'good' in 42% of cases, and 'very good' in another 18%). Looking at the results of the follow-up question, it would be fair to say that in the view of the social workers the development and behaviour of very few young people had been adversely affected by their placement in a children's home. While for many young people the effect of the home, as judged by social workers, had been at best 'neutral or mixed', for some, especially for their education and self-confidence, significant improvements were judged to have taken place.

About a third (32.1%) of the young people had been placed in a children's home because of potential or actual abuse and a further third had been placed there on account of their behaviour. Only 6 of the 43 young people in the 'abused' group were destined in the care plan to return to the parental home. In fact, the care plans included a return to the parental home for very few (23.1%) of the young people. Instead, it was planned that just under a third (30.6%) would go to foster care and a similar proportion (29.1%) would go into independent living.

During their stay in a home, young people had contact with their families but the frequency of this was largely determined by the distance of the children's home from the family home. Overall, nearly four out of ten (38.1%) of the families lived 20 miles or more away from the home. However, this was particularly so for the families of young people living in independent homes, two-thirds of which lived more than 20 miles away compared with just under a quarter (23.6%) of the families of young people living in local authority homes. Not surprisingly, there was a direct but negative relationship between frequency of contact and distance from the family home – in short, the greater the distance the less the contact. We have noted elsewhere (Gibbs and Sinclair 1998) that, putting aside the difficulties of contact between young people and their families, the location of some homes well away from the family home and neighbourhood could have positive effects. Not least of these would be a limitation on some of the previous contacts that had proved a negative influence on the behaviour of young people and had on occasions tempted them into delinquency.

Like the young people, 80 per cent of whom had said the placement had 'helped' them, over three-quarters (77.6%) of the social workers were happy that the current placement was the right one.

5. Key variations across the samples

We called one of our previous publications *Children's Homes: A Study in Diversity* (Sinclair and Gibbs 1998a), a description that still holds for the homes, the staff and the young people in the present study. A key example is the variation in the number of staff care hours. Table 2.8 demonstrates this with a measure based on the total of staff care hours divided by the number of children in the home at the time of the survey, and also with a related measure based on staff care hours divided by the number of beds the home is registered for. On both counts the variation is substantial.

Table 2.8 Variation in staff care hours available to residents

	Range	Mean	Median	Standard deviation
Care hours 1				
Total care staff hours by number of residents	37–254 hrs	83.4 hrs	71.5 hrs	52.2 hrs
Care hours 2				
Total care staff hours by number of registered beds	37–221 hrs	65.3 hrs	57.2 hrs	34.5 hrs

Source: *Details of Home Questionnaire* (*Staff* and *Current Resident Log* data).

Table 2.9 provides a further reminder of some of the other key variations that have featured or been touched upon in this short chapter. We do not wish to comment on every aspect of the table as to do so would only repeat earlier observations. However, two observations are pertinent. The first, and at the risk of labouring the point, there is considerable variation between homes. In many respects this is unsurprising because homes fulfil different functions and meet different needs. The second is that such variation has to be taken into account in the analysis presented in later chapters if fair comparisons are to be made and robust conclusions to be drawn.

Table 2.9 Further key variations in the samples

Area of variation	Variation/range
Building/home	
Type	Mid-Victorian house to purpose-built
Age of building	2–150 years
No. of reg. beds	1–10
The staff group	
Average age of staff group	30–49 years (overall 40 years)
% of females in staff group	31%–100% (overall 65%)
Average time staff group in post	4 months–11 years (overall 4.6 years)
Av. time staff group in res. work	3.1–19.7 years (overall 8.4 years)
% of staff group unqualified	9%–91% (overall 42%)
The resident group	
Average age of resident group	7–17 years (overall 13.8 years)
% females in resident group	0%–100%
Average stay of group in home	37–803 days (overall 352 days)
% of group – convictions before	0%–100% (overall 33%)
% of group – convictions during	0%–100% (overall 28%)
% of group – excluded before	0%–100% (overall 35%)
% of group – excluded during	0%–83% (overall 22%)
Average happiness score of group	13–92 (overall 56)
The staff – as individuals	
Ages	19–64 years (overall mean 39.7 years)
Time in home	1 month to 29 years
Time in residential work	1 month to 32 years

Continued on next page

Table 2.9 continued

Area of variation	Variation/range
The residents – as individuals	
Ages	7–17 years (overall mean 13.8 years)
Length of stay in home	6 days–4.3 years (mean 352 days)
Staffing variables	
Staff group views on staffing ratio:	
About right	12%–100% (overall 46%)
Too few staff	14%–100% (overall 53%)
Staff group assessment of leadership:	
Low	0%–100% (overall 33%)
Medium	0%–71% (overall 33%)
High	0%–100% (overall 33%)
Staff group satisfaction with job:	
Very satisfied/satisfied	0%–100% (overall 86%)
Very dissatisfied/dissatisfied	0%–100% (overall 14%)

Changes over time

Before drawing this chapter to a conclusion, we want to summarise some of the changes that took place over T1 and T2 (a period of about 10–12 months). Due to closure (two homes) and one authority's decision not to continue participation beyond T1 (two homes), we had four fewer homes in the study at T2. Table 2.10 indicates that a quarter of the homes at T1, but fewer at T2, reported a change in purpose and function over the preceding 12 months; however, a greater influence on continuity, for good or bad, was the number of homes where a different manager was in post at T2. Staff turnover appeared to be constant at about 25 per cent over the two periods, although the overall figures mask considerable variation between homes.

Although just over half (52%) of the young people in our study were no longer living in their original children's homes at T2, this is not unusual in a system where it is the intention to accommodate a proportion of them in this way for relatively short periods of time. However, what is not intended for these young people is that nearly four out of ten (38%) of them will have a new field social worker in the space of a year.

Table 2.10 Changes and variation to sample

Changes/variation	T1	T2
Number of homes in study	45 (30 LA; 15 Non-stat.)	41 (28 LA; 13 Non-stat.)
Number of homes reporting change in purpose and function in previous 12 months	11 of 41	3 of 28
Change of home's manager at T2 (LA homes only)	*Not applicable at T1*	11 of 28
Proportion of staff appointed in last 12 months	25.3%	25.4%
Number of young people no longer living at same home at T2	*Not applicable at T1*	118 of 226
Number of young people with different social worker at T2	*Not applicable at T1*	86 of 226
Number of young people with no allocated social worker	0	27 (incl. 4 'case closed') of 226

Summary

In this chapter we have set out and considered many of the features of homes, including the resources available to managers, which provide the 'structure' within which care takes place. As has been shown in numerous previous studies, children's homes are very varied places. We have explained how they differ in their basic characteristics (for example, their size), in the experience and characteristics of the staff, in the age, sex and social history of the residents, in the length of time the residents stay, and in the way the residents and staff perceive the home.

Arising from these differences are a number of concerns. These relate to:

1. *The young people living in children's homes.* In general, residents have complex histories, which in some cases are manifest in socially unacceptable behaviour. This finding reinforces the work of others

(Berridge and Brodie 1998; Sinclair and Gibbs 1998a; Whitaker *et al.* 1998). There is, therefore, the issue of whether these young people may negatively influence others and, in that event, how to work with their behaviour. Later in the book we shall see the ways in which managers are concerned with managing these behavioural issues. We will also look at how they differ in their approaches and whether these differences result in differences in cost and outcomes. It may be the case that young people in general are challenging. However, some homes look after more challenging children than others and this needs to be taken into account.

2. *Staffing.* This chapter shows that homes employ a mix of senior, and mostly trained, staff and younger, much less trained, staff. There is also a high turnover of staff. This implies that managers cannot rely on an ethos produced by pre-existing training for their younger staff. Previous work suggests that 'staff agreement' is a key issue. This in turn means that managers are likely to spend time in bringing this about. The high turnover of staff and the use of agency staff mean that training has to be, in part, an ongoing process.

3. *Staffing ratios.* We found considerable variation, a situation little changed since previous research in this area (Sinclair and Gibbs 1998a). In Chapter 7 we examine in greater detail the contribution of staffing costs in relation to overall costs.

4. *Buildings.* Here again the relevance is to costs – while previous work has indicated that there are major differences in the style of buildings used to provide residential care, we have limited understanding of how this relates to costs or the likely impact this may have on outcomes. Later in the book we are able to fill some of these gaps on the revenue costs of running the homes housed in different forms of buildings; we also relate the information to outcomes.

The purpose of this book is to examine the relationship between 'structure', 'process' and 'outcomes' – in short, to see how the variations outlined in this chapter combine with the practice of the manager and the costs of the home to produce a variety of outcomes. In the next chapter we begin a close examination of what managers of children's homes do – the process of managing a children's home.

Chapter 3

Creating, Maintaining and Influencing a Staff Team

Introduction

This chapter begins our description of the *process* of managing children's homes. It is the first of three chapters focusing on aspects of practice and its management that are common to all homes. As such, these three chapters pave the way for Chapter 6, where we arrive at a qualitatively grounded explanation of the features which actually differ in the management of homes. We provide a brief introduction to the qualitative part of the research as a preliminary to focusing on managers' work in relation to their staff teams.

Chapters 3, 4 and 5 focus on managers' roles in children's homes and their working relationships with staff and with the young people in their care. Our data sources are primarily threefold: interviews with managers of children's homes, group interviews with staff teams and open-ended responses from questionnaires.

The qualitative material addresses fundamental questions on which the research is based. How do managers prefer things to work, what do they do to achieve this, what approaches do they use, and what helps things to happen as they would like them to? What kinds of resources do managers feel they need in order to do the kinds of work they consider necessary? What structures are in place and utilised to enable the management of children's homes? How far is the management of homes shared, and is this synonymous with sharing the leadership of homes? What roles do managers of children's homes perform in relation to achieving good practice?

In formal terms, what managing a home entails is constructed increasingly by external forces, where external accountability drives the execution of the role (Department of Health 2002; TOPSS 2003). In interviewing the managers of the 40 homes available to us from the original sample of 45, we wanted to hear first-hand accounts of what the role entailed, what processes governed activity, what managers' intentions were and how things actually worked out.

Building on insights from previous work (Sinclair and Gibbs 1998a; Whitaker et al. 1998), we sought to identify the processes involved in establishing clear and successful work in five key practice arenas. These were: the manager's own role and identity, the manager in relation to the staff team, to the young people as individuals and as a group, to networks outside the boundary of the home, and to their own organisation. We aimed to obtain full accounts of what helped to sustain preferred ways of working. We also aimed to attain accounts of influences that prevented or hindered the achievement of declared goals and approaches to them. Where aspirations in relation to goals and approaches fell into patterns, we aimed to identify particular strategic ways of working.

The interview structure was developed from an interview schedule used successfully in earlier work (Sinclair and Gibbs 1998a), after assessing its reliability. Questions of low priority for the present project were omitted, and questions relevant to the managers' relationships with their own organisation, and their own preferred approaches to managing both staff and their practice, were added. Put simply, the interviews were designed to help us understand what constitutes good management practice, good leadership and the optimum ways of bringing both these about. We gathered data on how managers preferred things to work in their homes, what they did to achieve this and what helped things to happen as they would like. In doing this, we were able to highlight the communication, negotiation and self-management skills they needed to use, and the skills, characteristics and personal qualities required.

An introductory period allowed us to visit our participating organisations and meet senior staff, the managers of homes and, where possible, staff groups and groups of young people in order to set out the aims of the project and respond to questions about it. Following on from this, we carried out interviews by telephone, an increasingly popular medium in qualitative work, and one which was successfully used by one of the current team in previous work with managers of children's homes (Whitaker et al. 1998). Qualitative telephone interviews are known to provide advantages and disadvantages methodologically and in terms of the process of participation as well as the quality of material (Barriball et al. 1996; Carr and Worth 2001). The medium enabled us to tape-record highly focused and detailed accounts, including many examples of practice, from the managers concerned, and furthered our confidence in its relevance as a research tool for use with samples of professionals. We were able to explore likely distinctions between the eloquence of spoken accounts and actual behaviour by spending time in homes and by seeking additional viewpoints. Each interview was broken into two parts; the first, shorter interview set out to:

- gain insight into any relevant changes in the respect of the home, organisational structure, or resident group
- remind the respondent of the project aims
- spend time preparing for the more detailed orientation of the second session
- seek permission to tape-record the interview.

The second interview lasted for a minimum of one hour and was governed by a semi-structured interview schedule. This was sent in advance to the respondent, who was then able to prepare for the interview in whatever manner they felt suitable; some managers consulted with their staff groups, for example. Each interview was tape-recorded and later transcribed, and was rated by the interviewer for the 35 elements of practice covered. First-level analysis involved thematic content analysis. Second-level analysis involved each transcription being rated further from a grounded conceptualisation of positive leadership characteristics. In other words, how well managers were doing in certain areas was rated. For this, the initial evidence from the more detailed ratings was used in conjunction with the content analysis. The eight ratings plus one nominal category from this second-level analysis were taken forward into the statistical analyses, as will be seen in Chapters 7 and 8.

In parallel with the interviews with managers, we embarked on a series of visits to children's homes to talk to staff. We proposed to include eight homes at this stage; however, the number of homes was increased to ten, in line with the numbers of overall participating organisations and their keenness to take part. Our plans to achieve two detailed discussions with whole staff groups, followed by a feedback session, were achieved in five of the ten homes participating in this part of the study. Meetings in the other five homes were longer in duration, though fewer in number. Overall, time spent with each was comparable across eight of the homes.

The visits to children's homes were intended to enable us to spend time with staff, and to discuss their experiences and ways of working, particularly in relation to the ways that potential for practice is influenced by staff deployment. Discussions held during the visits focused on the use of staff time, the roles of staff, the role and approach of the manager of the home and the ways staff come to understand these, and examples from practice. These latter were elicited to highlight the interplay of influential variables such as the role of external management, the approach and expectations of the manager of the home, the use of resources and the working philosophy of the staff group.

Questionnaires to staff at T1, as discussed in Chapter 2, provided space for open-ended comments on the consequences of leadership in their experience, the consequences of levels of staffing, the availability and use of resources, and any other related comments.

These three interlinking data sources provided a suitably fertile body of material for corroboration and analysis. We use the different forms of material together here in order to describe ways of working in children's homes. From this description we examine where differences lie in what managers of homes are able to achieve. This prepares the ground for explaining these differences.

Our qualitative analysis was extensive and followed established techniques (Patton 1980; Seale 1999; Strauss 1987). This allowed us to present here detailed and discursive material, which we hope conveys perspectives, highlights understandings and enables readers to situate themselves in relation to the viewpoint being expressed. Our main points emerged through 'successively evolving interpretations' (Strauss 1987) and we have selected quotations from across the range of respondents in order to illustrate these points. This is distinct from choosing quotations in line with frequency of occurrence. Thus weight emerges during the course of our analysis rather than from the number of times a specific idea was mentioned and/or the numbers of managers who mentioned it.

The style of data collection encouraged extensive accounts and these we have used to illuminate our organised descriptions of what takes place throughout Chapters 3, 4 and 5. As such, the quotations are integral to the points being made, not least because they give voice to practice-based viewpoints. The respondents' voice was central to this strand of the research (Rubin and Rubin 2005). Although difficult to break into narratives and preserve the integrity of what was being said, where indicated quotations have been shortened to avoid repetition within and occasionally where digression or interruption occurred. We are unable to convey the enthusiastic way in which many managers provided their accounts, but we are confident that their thoughtful commitment is self-evident.

We begin by extensively focusing on accounts from five different homes, which will act as springboards for describing our findings. Quotations are given as illustrations of key points. The identity of those quoted has been protected throughout this and subsequent chapters. While respondents may think they recognise their own contributions, it is likely to be the case that the particular quotation was from a manager working in a children's home located many miles away – a situation we have encountered many times in our dissemination of this work.

Preliminary examples

Two managers of different homes look back to when first they came into role in their specific homes:

> Just my first point was about trying to assess people's value base really, how much did they like kids and how much did they just say that they liked kids and how much could they work with behaviours that really at times are quite [pause] quite appalling, quite distressing, violent confrontational behaviour, how do they manage that and still come back in the next day and how are they able to focus specifically. The ability to focus on feelings and needs rather than on behaviours and that I think breaks down the old school [traditional residential social workers] from what we need to be doing now.

> My philosophy is that people must be committed and they go that extra mile with the young person to get a positive outcome – you want to try and instil standards, you try and be an appropriate role model and young people and staff teams learn by that, or you hope they learn by that, and the standards that you're trying to bring about in all of them, they need to consolidate [these] and work as a group.

Both these managers identified some of the spirit they were trying to bring about from the earliest stages of work, and some of the values they were trying to inculcate. Next, two members of staff directly comment on their experiences of being managed, which differ considerably, in their respective homes:

> Leadership [here] is inspiring to fellow workers to strive to achieve best outcomes for young people. Leadership is firm but fair, anti-discriminatory, empowering and open. Some staff however do not like to be managed and cannot live up to the expectations the manager requires. This can lead to friction within the staff team. Regular supervision and staff meetings take place. Manager [is] very good at delegating tasks and giving workers 'ownership' of their own duties. Many management tasks

are administrative and require a sound knowledge of form filling and chasing down paperwork rather than 'hands-on' child care. Approx two-thirds of all paperwork has nothing to do with care management. [It's] Very frustrating and time consuming. My manager possesses very good people skills, coupled with sound working practice and practical knowledge of child care and lots of experience which cannot be gained from courses and qualifications, i.e. graduate managers with no experience only theories. My manager invests a lot in the hope of getting a lot back from those below.

Our current unit manager tends to lead by dictating how things should be done. On occasion he does ask our views, but usually has his mind made up prior to this. He tends to analyse why young people behave the way they do, which is useful, but does not give direction on how to deal with and handle this behaviour. Child care management [external] tends to scapegoat care staff when things go wrong. I'm happy to be accountable for the decisions I make but not what happens when I'm not there.

All four accounts show us something about the standards managers set; the second and third accounts tell us a little about different ways of bringing about compliance with their expectations. The fifth account here is from a long-experienced manager, who reflects on what has worked well:

Having a staff team like the one I work with makes my role as a manager so much easier. The initial work forming, storming and norming has really paid off. I value my staff and I let them know it; this for me inspires the most fruitful results. I manage by example and empower my team by involving everyone in everything I can. Times demand flexibility and I have encouraged a love of 'change for the better' and when we are in chaos we cope and get there in spite of it. As a manager I listen to my team and they in turn listen to each other; the celebration of this is we all listen to the young people. I am proud of the achievements of my front-line troops, a group who form a great part of my own personal and professional development.

These quotations were selected to represent and illustrate crucially important levels of task when getting to grips with managing a children's home. Aspects of this involved forming and maintaining a dependable staff team with a similar value base and commitment to caring for young people. Teams had to work to high standards, be able to learn from others, be consistent in their practice and worthy of respect. Managers had to be capable of setting an example and bringing about a working commitment to expectations, some of which related to fulfilling bureaucratic requirements. We have assigned these areas of practice and their management to three interlinking categories:

- creating, maintaining and influencing a staff team (Chapter 3)
- shaping and maintaining the role of manager within the context of the wider organisation (Chapter 4)
- shaping and maintaining work in relation to the needs of young people (Chapter 5).

What follows here is a description of these aspects and of the interplay between them. Our aim in these three chapters is to illustrate the way homes are managed and leadership is formed by managers and their teams as part of a sequence of development experiences: the *process* of managing a children's home.

Ways of creating, maintaining, and influencing a staff team

Included in this chapter are: the nature of the manager's post; getting to know staff resources, needs and characteristics; establishing the role of manager in relation to the team; making staffing changes; developing the capability of the staff group; sharing roles and responsibilities with staff; helping staff to be autonomous; and maintaining and supporting the staff team.

The nature of the manager's post

We asked each manager to describe how they came into their current post. In so doing, we wanted to know about the legacies each encountered, what if anything managers felt needed changing, and how they went about achieving the changes they thought necessary. These early beginnings with staff teams provided highly influential experiences.

Each manager had their own unique experience of appointment and coming into post, and in most cases early experiences were where the boundaries for and tone of practice were set: the ensuing potential for practice was established at an early point in managers' experience with their staff team.

Of the 40 homes whose managers were interviewed from our original sample of 45, 33 had managers appointed as permanent, while seven were working in temporary posts. Eleven of the managers had 'risen through the ranks' in their home, and ten of these managers' posts had been 'acting' roles prior to being made into permanent positions. Many of those managers who had fulfilled 'acting' roles had experienced long periods of uncertainty prior to attaining full or permanent status.

Some of the temporary posts were acting as bridging solutions – for example, until a permanent appointment could be made, or while the permanent manager had been seconded to another job. Others were awaiting policy decisions about the future of the home or its permanent manager. With the exception of four homes where the manager's role was shared formally over three hierarchical tiers, nine homes shared their managers in some way and three of these were temporary arrangements of unspecified duration.

For non-permanent managers, knowing how long they were expected by their parent organisation to be in post influenced in part their clarity of vision and way forward. Although working at times with short-term goals only, most non-permanent managers were committed to managing their homes as though their interests were long term, and personal pride played a high part in this. Perhaps the clearest role brief given by the organisation was also the least specific and yet afforded the fullest autonomy, and often the highest degree of proffered external support. This was where a manager was newly appointed as a temporary measure in order to redeem or turn around a home where there had been extreme forms of difficulty. This placed high reliance on the abilities of managers to get to grips with the emergent situation, put their own stamp on the home and claim their own direction for it.

Eleven managers occupied posts in homes where changes in purpose and function across the organisation had taken place over the previous 12 months; many more had experienced three or more clear changes in purpose and function during their time in post. Planned shifts were liable to influence potential for practice in a negative manner where managers were not involved in realistic timetabling of clear changes in task; this was a frequent occurrence. For example, impending changes might mean that pressure to admit young people was experienced in respect of the anticipated rather than current remit. The ensuing form of gradual shift held potential for a concomitant lack of clarity in ways of working with the group of young people who were likely to have quite different needs. The work of a mixed-sex, long-term provision, for example, may have been about to change to that of a pre-fostering home. The ability to protect the home against the strain of trying to meet a high mix of complex needs varied according to placement demand, external perceptions of the state of the home and the established reputation of the manager. Retaining clarity in role in the face of fundamental changes often fell to the manager to negotiate locally and organise around.

Many managers found themselves in situations where tolerance of uncertainty over long periods was required, whether it was in respect of their own role or that of the home. Clearly, this meant that containment of anxiety, apprehension and resistance to change formed a large part of what they had to manage both with and for the staff and residents.

Most of the 'acting' roles had existed as such due to pending changes within the wider organisation – where corresponding vertical shifts in personnel meant that the previous manager's return to work would be in doubt for some reason, or where there was some sort of redeeming brief for the temporary manager to attempt to turn around a home that had been spiralling downwards over time. Similar reasons for this lack of permanency were given by managers whose posts at the time of interview were temporary in some way.

As noted previously, rising through the ranks and being given temporary status as a children's home manager was not an unusual occurrence. Although this was indeed a way of enculturing managers into the way a home operates, such a state was not always desired by the organisation, particularly if negative events, such as staff suspension or long-term sickness, had preceded the new appointment. The point at which managers came newly into role most often represented a period when some sort of change in the purpose and function of the home or its culture was under review. A new manager often provided an opportunity to bring about major shifts in either purpose or approach:

> The way the [previous] manager was – he had a massive effect on the staff team and he was, it was quite oppressive and it is a really sensitive area and I've got a majority of female members of staff who he really bullied and intimidated. So there was an added pressure there for me to sort of come in softly, very softly if you like.

For those who occupied an acting status, whether past or current, there was a rather tentative authority in the manager's role and along with this came a lack of clarity in respect of their own role and expectations from the wider organisation. As one manager shows:

> So [after two and a half years] it became less of caretaking it and more that this was my home to run, though that wasn't formalised until just last week.

Sometimes this worked to good effect in relation to providing continuity:

> But I was, seemed to be consistent through that [change in management] because I was the Assistant Manager or Acting Senior for all that time and, to be quite honest, at the time when the post became vacant it seemed like a natural progression.

Newly appointed managers had to bridge old and new circumstances and form their own way of working in relation to each. Where managers were temporarily appointed against an uncertain future, the extent to which they were able to establish positive control, even though they were fully responsible, was debatable. When all those involved were adjusting to new responsibilities, designations and approaches, the extent to which transition to the role of manager could be achieved efficiently and effectively from a temporary base was in question. Status of post at the point of transition was clearly important.

Knowing staff resources, needs and characteristics

In our sample, it was rarely the case that a manager was employed to work with a home from its inception. In the two instances where this had occurred, the manager was able to shape the team and set the context for work from the earliest stage, and therefore felt a high degree of ownership and responsibility:

> Although I had child care staff and a domestic I didn't have a deputy until [four] months later, so I was actually very resident at that time and very resident here until the May which, looking back…was quite a good thing because we all settled in very well together.

It is worthwhile noting here a point that we will emphasise throughout – i.e. that forming and maintaining a staff team was continuous and sensitive work. Whatever work took place in respect of shaping a staff team, influencing their practice, forming relationships with young people and with networks surrounding the home, and the majority of other forms of work, more than just 'topping up' attention was needed. As situations changed and membership of staff groups and groups of young people fluctuated, the process of bringing the groups together had to be revisited, not least because there were attendant shifts in interpersonal dynamics and relationships.

It was most usually the case that managers were employed in posts where a set of difficulties posed particular issues with which to begin work. The initial brief given to some managers was to create a stable environment and, in effect, to redeem the home, sometimes in the face of dissatisfaction within the local community. This was a frequently encountered situation for managers in the sample, requiring intensive work with the team:

> Team meetings and individual supervision, individual supervisions were very important, particularly for the staff who didn't know me. I spent a lot of time telling them something about myself, how I worked, what I

expected and, team meetings to try and pull everyone together. A lot of, a lot of input…a lot of support, being around a lot of the time as well because the staff were very shaky.

In another organisation, where the permanent manager was away on long-term sickness leave, we can see a similar situation:

[I came] just as people were being told the results of some of the suspensions and stuff, people had moved. So picking up quite a bit of slack I suppose… Obviously the staff team didn't know who I was, where I'd come from, background, anything really, I was sort of sprung on them really, who the hell are you, where have you come from, sort of touch. But that was fine. So it was only going to be, initially, we thought for about six weeks and that's just gone on and on and on and on and I'm still here.

In the majority of cases, newly taking over a home meant that managers had to spend time acquainting themselves with both staff and young people (and vice versa) and starting to build relationships *before* being able to look at the overall direction of the home in respect of its place in the wider organisation. Much of the practice in children's homes centred around forming positive relationships and boundaries, and much of the management of practice focused on establishing mechanisms for communication and monitoring. Becoming familiar with groups of staff and young people was of high priority, and the most usual immediate concern.

Part of this familiarisation was to identify needs of some kind. While care plans and residential plans accompanied the young people as a record of their needs, little existed on paper as a record of staff skills, abilities, personal characteristics and approaches. Changes in Codes of Practice and Registration are in hand currently for residential workers. It remains the case that, unlike other practice situations that require a professional qualification and an established skills base prior to appointment, staff in children's homes, with suitable police checks in place, can practise if motivated and appointed so to do. Particular skills cannot be guaranteed. In respect of their staff teams, managers of homes needed to spend time getting to know their staff members and understanding their experience, abilities, limitations, attitudes and approaches; they also needed to be interested in their general well-being. This was part of being able to gain confidence in their team members and to understand how best to deploy them in order for them to work well together. A similar position was experienced by staff, who had to be confident in each others' skills and responses to difficult situations in order to practise well. From time to time and most especially at the early stages of a manager coming into post, neither managers nor staff were secure in being able to predict what their work contexts would be like.

In cases where the manager had been promoted from within the home, the process of becoming a manager was more a matter of re-establishing oneself with a new identity and an appropriate level of authority:

> As the new manager, I already had a relationship with staff it took me six months to become *not* a member of staff.

As we have seen, establishing this was doubly hard to achieve where managers were promoted from within the home on an 'acting' basis. Often rivalries emerged. A manager whose authority was proving to be problematic and unacceptable for one member of staff comments:

> That person is still finding it very hard that I'm [now] her manager. So I'm still getting a lot of playing games and a lot of poor me, myself and I… and I really have supported this person and it's been very hard.

Getting the pace of bringing about changes, and therefore staff adjustment to the newly designated person, was an important consideration.

Establishing the role of manager in relation to the team

Managers in this project were always mindful of the impact they were having when newly appointed:

> You have to be very careful and very sensitive in how you manage that because nobody wants to see somebody coming in and changing everything around, even if you, straight away you don't feel it's right. You have to do it in a very sensitive and productive way really and that is the same for the staff because their anxieties are high, you know. Any change, but a change in management is very difficult for staff and, you've got the staff who are out to please and the staff who are thinking, well I'm not doing that. So you have to manage it in a very sensitive way… but it's about obviously bringing them on board – you have to give them something.

Staff teams had to be taken along with managers rather than pushed into agreement with new approaches:

> I just worked with what I found and stuck to what I believed in and kind of knew that they were going to have to get to know me before they were going to trust me and I didn't come in with the attitude 'I'm the boss so therefore they've got to trust me', I think it was about relationship-building with them. I needed to get to know them as well as they needed to get to know me and the one thing that I do pride myself in, without

sounding big-headed, I was always very astute at being able to judge problems, issues and people and I think that's why I always get on so well with the kids because I can be frank with them and quite honest.

Establishing the appropriate speed at which to work in relation to making changes in approach or practice was a matter for careful judgement because its impact could be widespread or non-existent:

I was aware because I'd been in a position as well where someone else came in and took over a unit and they were a little bit dictatorial – 'you will' and 'we don't' – and to some extent rubbished a lot of the practice itself, rubbished some of the things we'd done for years, and I think because I didn't want to do that, I did get a bit wishy washy at times and uncertain. I can see that now, because, I don't know, I don't want to threaten people that way, and that, I just don't think that's me, I just couldn't really do that. And yes, there are times and places I think it would be much easier just to be able to go 'do this' (laughing) and then I think, it might be for that ten minutes but it wouldn't be [so] a week or a month down the line.

Establishing one's own identity as manager paved the way for being able to claim ownership of the staff team.

Making staffing changes

Getting the right personnel in place was seen to be vital. Often the staff whom managers inherited were not the staff that they felt the home and its purpose and function required. Sometimes staff did not act in line with the preferred approach of the manager, other times resistance to change was such a major obstacle to progress that staffing had to be reappraised. Moving on 'old' staff and bringing in new staff members were seen as challenging for everyone concerned, although in many cases such changes did represent some of the most important transitions in feeling to own the team:

I suppose it was weighing up…what had been tried before [I arrived] was the sort of big stick approach, that hadn't worked, what you have to do sometimes, within residential care, I think you get to a point where people have to move on for their own development and sanity sometimes but they need a bit of a push or they need some encouragement in that, and I suppose what I've done is encouraged people to look at other things and say 'Well, look, you know, are you gonna do this job forever, do you think your heart's really in it, how about looking at other things?' rather than 'You're doing a crap job, you know, I'm taking you down the poor performance route', all those sorts of options if you like. Because you then get people's backs up and they stay, they stay just because they're not going to be bullied into doing whatever and I think that's fair. I've employed people that I feel have got what I want for the unit with the same sort of ideas and personalities that, that would fit.

Making difficult staffing changes capably were part of proving one's worth as manager and inspiring confidence and trust in shaping the overall direction of the home. Taking into consideration the impact such changes had on the remaining staff group and on the kinds of care which could be provided sometimes outweighed the benefits of the change itself:

> I still think we've got a lot of work to do… I feel in some senses we're turning the corner but there is, there is a couple of members of staff who have really stayed still in their work, who are resistant to change or who pay lip service to change, which very quickly will revert to old ways, particularly in times of difficulty, the old ways are the best and they can't see anything positive, when you've got a really negative situation when the home's up in the air bouncing, the kids are being really negative, they can't see a positive way to lead these young people out of it. It's very much 'Right, close everything down, you get nothing, that's it, finished, we'll react to whatever you throw at us' and it's really difficult trying to manage that out within the staffing crisis we're having because the same members of staff, once challenged about practice, are very liable to go off sick and that is, that is devastating to us if that happens. The last thing I need is a new face coming in, every single day, for the young people not to know who's going to be on shift in the morning, that's, you know, very destabilising for them.

For the manager quoted here, the current situation would be redeemed when an imminent increase in staff numbers occurred. This would mean that she expected to be able to 'soak up sickness and it'll come down to direct challenge'. She would be able to be more direct in her challenge without being fearful of the likely consequence of staff absence, which would produce ultimately further disturbances associated with bringing in temporary staff.

It was interesting to note that keeping the home staffed with familiar faces was a preference expressed across the whole sample – the impact of changes in personnel was regarded as ultimately negative for the young people, and to be guarded against. The net effect of this was that when staff absence through sickness or holidays arose, many staff worked excessive hours of overtime, either paid for or taken as time off in lieu, which in turn generated difficulties by contributing to exhaustion, strain and unwieldy rotas.

Developing the capability of the staff group

Managers usually approached their job by direct involvement in practice, role modelling, educating practice, assuring consistency and generally making sure tasks were done in their preferred way. A large part of this relied on being able to motivate staff, bring energy to the task and at the same time provide security by taking responsibility for the home. Being clear about their expectations of staff was an important starting point for managers in developing the staff team:

> It's a benevolent dictatorship. If I have knowledge that I think will inform good practice I share it, there is no point in me having it and being Superwoman, because there are not enough hours in the day for me to achieve all the things I would have to achieve. So if I have knowledge about good practice, if I have ideas I try and generate debate and discussion across the staff, and what I think my role is about, I interpret essential government requirements, legislation, etc., and try and set a tone and set a working ethos for staff to work within to provide good service outcomes for young people. I ask my team leaders, my two deputies, to take on board those issues and lead the team to meet the aims and objectives of our organisation in relation to service delivery. I ask the team to ensure the well-being day-to-day of children and adolescents is taken care of to the best of their ability and I can dip in and out of any of those functions, but there are not enough hours in the day and not enough for me to be able to achieve it all in one go. So it is collaboration, you know, I set standards and expectations for children to achieve, I set them for the staff as well, cos if the staff, you know, they're my tools to do the job I do. If I was a carpenter these would be my hammers and nails. So I have to take very, very good care of my tools to ensure that what I believe is good child care practice occurs.

Helping staff to learn was achieved in a variety of ways. Being clear on direction and following this by monitoring what takes place was often seen as a way to encourage growth:

> I just allowed myself to stick to what I believed in and worked with them [staff] in a way that was, not dictatorial but, but quite clear that on certain issues that this was the way we were going. I encouraged group discussion, I encouraged group ownership, because I felt that that was the best way forward... But I believe a manager's got to allow staff to learn and grow and do things. If you do it all for them they never learn, they never develop. So it's about giving them responsibilities and allowing them to achieve those without a lot of interference, as long as it's not detrimental

or they're making such a cock-up that you need to [pause] intervene in a more proactive way.

Aiding individual learning was a major part of the manager's task. It had its attendant difficulties in terms of time and resource commitment:

So [in the beginning] we had our one staff meeting we spent just going over a particular incident and how we might have dealt with it differently to, in order to, not to put anybody down but to look at alternative methods of, of intervention and timing and what went wrong and what went right. So it's those sorts of things that I'm trying to get them to understand, to use their brains in a much more lateral way than just narrow sort of channels. So that takes time and every staff team's different and, and there's all different levels of experience and it's quite interesting watching them develop.

However, this was not regarded as the sole responsibility of managers; rather it was supported by other members of staff, and importantly, by training sections. Staff were not always receptive to formal training, and managers sometimes had to think creatively about how to achieve this:

The biggest resistance was going to training courses because they were frightened because they hadn't been and they said that they didn't know anything and so I brought the training into the house and I had it delivered to the team as a whole and I had, I've had staff who never uttered a word at the start who now, by two years on actually love those days and contribute fully. So to me that's really, that's been great.

In addition to the potential alienating effects of training for those already doing the job for which training was being provided, the work-based nature of National Vocational Qualification (NVQ) training presented difficulties in respect of freeing-up staff time and having sufficient assessors available. The way managers developed staff as members of their team was felt to be their particular responsibility. Part of establishing the team involved helping members to gain knowledge of organisational concepts, structure, procedures and an overall sense of 'how we do things here'. This in turn required managers to have a clear view as to the goals being worked towards, sufficient confidence with their teams to be emphatic without stifling staff contributions, such that the effect was a shared motivation and ownership of the goals and steps towards achieving them. In this process, something of a balancing act was required, as managers had to be able to judge timing on when things could be shared effectively – i.e. soon enough to inspire a sense of ownership, but not so soon that members of staff lacked confidence or stretched their practice beyond their capabilities or the bounds of safety.

Sharing roles and responsibilities with staff

Routine tasks were most often allocated across the staff team, and this provided a starting point for helping staff to feel valuable as individuals within the team. Being able to designate tasks was not the same as being able actually to share roles and responsibilities within the home. Tasks could be supervised or monitored in some way. Sharing roles and responsibilities involved greater insight into staff capabilities and a corresponding trust in team members. This was partly developed by working alongside each other and experiencing each others' reactions, partly by being open in commenting on performance and learning from it. Being able to take criticism from one's peers without it being seen as a personal slight was an important skill to develop:

> You need to know the person next to you is not undermining your efforts so you've got to have that trust and trust takes a long time to establish. But in residential care, as professionals – I expect the children to take some time in trusting us – but as adults, you've got to buy that straight away, and that professional criticism allows that trust to develop. Because 'I told you that I didn't like how you dealt with that child and these are the reasons why, and now let's get on with the job', you know, rather than 'Oh, saying something nasty about me, I can't work with her on Thursday'.

When staff were in place with whom managers were confident, the path to achieving preferred ways of operating became clearer. Managers frequently emphasised the way that their staff teams determined their own potential:

> You're only as good as your staff team, and if you haven't got a good staff team then you've got lots of problems really. So to enable you to have a good staff team you have to empower them and you have to get them to believe in their abilities and their skills… It's just about managers being able to nurture that [skill] and develop people's skills and giving them confidence.

Of great importance were senior staff. These were seen as holding high influence over direct practice, particularly where part of their role involved supervising other members of the team:

> I really do believe that senior residential social workers have the biggest say in the culture of the home. They're the lead person actually on the

shift, working with the young people and to get the right seniors in is perhaps the most important thing…by getting those sort of people in the position where they are shift leaders that feeds down into the rest of the staff team… I can then, when I'm using seniors when we do our supervision, that's where I put my values and principles and discuss those sorts of things with the seniors and tell them how I would like to see the shifts being run and how I would like to see this culture develop; it's making sure you have a strong management structure that allows the other staff to give them a clear focus really about what is expected of them and what are the right things to do and what are the wrong things to do.

Senior staff had to be able reliably to transmit and maintain managers' value bases, which included some aspects of knowledge, understanding, ways of thinking, skills and, importantly, disposition. Sharing different functions, according to the situation and strengths of each staff member, became effective when the worth of each individual became apparent. This was especially important in respect of senior staff, who were in many cases part of the support system which managers drew upon for themselves. Using senior staff to influence changes in approach or practice was seen as part of a suitably paced strategy to bring about ownership and ultimately empowerment within the home:

It's keep chipping away at a very low level. It's about, you know – rather than me trying to formally effect change in them by sitting them down in supervision and saying 'This is what you must do' which, for these people [pause] would be, you know, they'd resist that change, it's about using staff meetings and using seniors and other more positive members of staff who, who are heading in the right direction to make sure they lead the shifts and lead those people through it.

Sharing roles and responsibilities was not a matter of the immediate delegation of tasks through formal channels. Certain characteristics had to be in place before sharing could be reliably achieved in order to attain consistency within the staff team. It was not always the case that senior staff were reliable sources of support. Some managers relied on the external support provided by other managers of homes rather than relying on their assistant managers for either support or to take decisions in their absence. Although some managers shared their roles, this most usually took the form of sharing tasks and some aspects of decision making, rather than sharing their positions as leaders within the home. Managers retained the exclusive authority to decide how far to share roles, largely because they were held uniquely accountable for their homes:

> I have never been a person that owns something solely to the point that it couldn't be fine tuned and I wouldn't listen to legitimate and reasonable and rational sorts of reasons for changing slightly. So that will always be an open book and I'm more than willing to listen to better ideas and going down an avenue of trying something slightly different. But the core and the essence of, of empowering children and making their lives better and giving them more positive choices will never ever leave me, and so therefore as long as the house practises that then basically the ownership is all of us but if it doesn't, if it looks like it's going off course then I'm going to grab it back very quickly. Because it's a reflection on me and I don't want to be reflected as someone who doesn't care.

As this example shows, part of the manager's role involves being open to finding alternative ways of achieving goals. Part of it also is to keep activity within defined purposes. Some sharing and delegation was an inevitable result of the increasing demands placed on managers' time from a senior level within the wider organisation:

> There's a lot more expected of me. My role has changed in the last five years and certainly in the last 18 months the expectation from my managers about my job, my role have definitely changed, and I'm delighted at that because I'm now more involved in the strategic planning processes, looking at induction programmes, looking at policies and procedures. Now I can't be doing that and coming into here and running the show. So my seniors are now doing all those daily routine tasks that I don't do any more. So there's been a shift in responsibilities if you like. Now that's been a culture shock for my seniors because I'm having to say 'but my expectation now is very different of your role than it was'.

And some of the sharing of responsibility was more a matter of being able to rely on the experience of other staff and their availability:

> [We've] taken five staff on at once. But they're five inexperienced people, never been in that situation before and although they were provided with a very good induction which was the first time ever and, you know, that was another sort of real positive thing but they still kept, there's no preparation for what you encounter in a residential establishment, even the most, even if you give them the most graphic scenarios and, and whatever, there's nothing that really prepares them for when they actually experience it and face it. And so you've still got, from the permanent members of staff who shift lead, they're still having to hold, run the shift but also troubleshoot and guide. The [new] staff are usually very nervous, they come to the shift leader asking every single question, it's highly pressured. We've

got some very, very difficult children, very difficult. We've had periods, long periods of violence and aggression and so when staff are taking that constantly and they're also under pressure on shift in terms of, you know, all of the decision making and role modelling and everything and just being always on the floor, it takes its toll really.

Both situations illustrate that, although the manager seems to retain a directive stance, residential staff were at times responsible for areas of practice that would have been the domain of the manager previously. Changes in role meant considerable time would be spent in re-educating staff members; this, coupled with changes in personnel, led to a very shifting environment:

It's hard because we've got one assistant manager who acts up at the moment and we've got another who will be leaving in the summer so we have new people coming into post. Now I think you kind of start again. The assistant managers who've been there for some time now are very, feel very clear and confident about their roles but in a sense because their roles are [going to be] all different, they all have different leads, it takes time for someone to sort of feel they've quite got hold of it.

In such an environment roles are dynamically interlinked and therefore all are affected by change in any one area. In this way, managers' roles involved integration and education as part of a rolling activity. At times this functioned well as a shared process, where existing staff members enjoined newcomers into the team. Success here depended on the equilibrium of the team overall, and the ability of team members to provide feedback to each other:

The relationships are there, I think everyone knows how everyone works, no one has any qualms about, you know, addressing any issues with each other and they can do that in a professional manner and then get on with the job in hand, you know, without any hostility between.

I expect my staff to professionally challenge each other and professionally criticise each other, and I've worked a long time now, for about two years on [this], when we professionally criticise each other, it's not personal. Don't run off and boo-hoo in the loos, it's not a personal attack, it's a professional challenge. And it's taken them some time to learn… And building that, you know, it's all about trust and respect for each other and consistency among the team. They're the things I'm trying to nurture and foster with the adults because I think they transfer beautifully into the work for service users.

Establishing a context for work which was seen to be fair to all members of staff was a vital part of the process:

So I think all in all it's trying to be as fair as possible with people but at the same time not suffer fools gladly, so, and I'm not one that manages from a buddy system, I always manage from a [pause] – you treat them all fairly and you don't have favourites and you don't make it obvious that you have favourites. You might respect some people even more highly than others but you don't let that interfere with what should be done and how it should be done when somebody is in need of correction or in need of guidance or whatever, and I think that, that's helped a lot really.

Helping staff to be autonomous

It was considered important to work collaboratively with staff, and as can be seen earlier, more experienced staff were relied upon to share tasks and to take responsibilities, where these were devolved. Staff autonomy was something to be worked towards, and was 'granted' as part of a process, rather than assumed to occur by right. It was rarely fully given. Although many managers liked most things to be 'run past' them in terms of decisions made within the home, others were turned to more frequently than they would have liked:

> So I think I've had to do a lot of trying to empower people to be able to make decisions and say 'Look, you know, I'm here to check out things rather than I'm here to, they make the decisions, oh I'm here to ratify things' and I think that is much, much better for the young people because they actually don't see me as either Santa Claus or the big stick, what they see me as, they see the core staff where the power should be, appropriate power should be, to actually make the decisions for, in the best interests of themselves and the young people.

Achieving a balance between being an empowering enabler of staff and being able to retain decision-making authority within the home was a fundamental part of the manager's role:

> I like to involve all of the staff in all the decision making and that's down to referrals and everything. So, basically, we discuss everything as a team, although they do accept and respect the fact that if [pause], if I need to make a decision that's different to theirs then I will do.

Often managers were cautious in allocating key worker or link worker roles to new staff members, preferring to wait until staff were encultured into the home. For inexperienced staff this was often a matter of working for an identifiable period in the home, and previously experienced staff were cases for the manager's individual judgement. Staff in these situations co-worked as key workers in order to gain experience. While key workers themselves were usually seen as the person of first resort for young people, their work was most usually regarded as taking place under the supervision of a senior member of staff. This illustrates one of the most crucial aspects of ways managers and staff groups work together – i.e. as an interdependent collaborative culture, led and developed by the manager within a hierarchical system of accountability. The interdependency between staff and managers was emphasised repeatedly, and sharing decisions while retaining accountability was the most frequently adopted position by managers:

> I know that they [staff] feel more comfortable when I'm around and I make them feel safe and secure. It's easy to make decisions when your manager is around because essentially you take some of the responsibility for that decision. If anything's going wrong, well, you know, there's somebody who will take that responsibility I suppose. Having said that I've got no question, no problems with the decisions that are made when I'm not here either. We talk about decisions that we make… I front it, front what we do very strongly and, you know, we're all involved in decisions too.

Staff autonomy was seen as being gained as part of a process, on the basis of prior experience being achieved. Although autonomous practice was thought of in positive terms, execution of tasks was within the boundaries of accountability, and feedback and communication, which meant that practice was not free-standing, were vital aspects of performance.

Maintaining and supporting the staff team

As might be reasonably anticipated in an interdependent team-based organisation, all managers of children's homes set a high premium on 'good communication'. Losing sight of what was taking place in the home was considered to be risk-taking practice. Keeping pace with the home involved the use of formal channels for handovers, staff meetings and supervision, to attain both consistency in team practice and insight into how things were for the young people.

Formal channels were highly valued but were supplemented by informal mechanisms, which were often more consistent than some of the more formal mechanisms. Formal mechanisms varied between homes in the extent to which they were subverted by pressures of some kind. Often informal exchanges were seen to provide opportunities for on-the-spot coaching, or monitoring:

People are very comfortable talking to me outside of supervision, and now nobody has to wait for supervision any more. I like to create a space for honest exchange, and I'm where I want to be with that now – staff come to me and say 'I'm a little bit worried about so and so'; concerns about peers are brought to me if staff think they can't raise this directly with their colleagues.

Finding a way of supervising which fitted every supervisory need was regarded as difficult. We give at length the next quotation. Here, the manager draws links between the ways that managers are familiar with the work of their staff by virtue of the nature of the task, what takes place in supervision, and the difficulty of 'finding a model that works' for supervision and making space for this:

The traditional model of supervision, you know, two hours, once every two or three weeks, it doesn't work in a res unit like that. Because the team works day in day out, holding each others' hands, working through crisis, working through good times, planning this, doing this, responding to this, responding to that, it's not like the field model where you go off and you do your work and you come back and you report to your supervisor what you've been doing. I know what my staff are doing day in day out because I'm there, and I'm getting that feedback all the time… We do then give formal time with a formal set agenda, the staff don't bring their own agenda, there is a formal agenda and we talk about things like the qualitative and quantitative elements of our work, inputs, outputs, efforts, achievements, outcomes, yeah, not only for the children we're working with but as team members, yeah. Through supervision sessions we talk about the training needs of people, yeah, and that's brought to another forum where we look at that. Supervision is about the staff, they're feeling, how they're feeling, are there any team issues, are there any unit issues they need the team leaders to pick up and take forward. So it's more the kind of, it's not the nitty gritty stuff, it's more things that become more problematic, less easy to address there and then, right, and the time to express them. But one of our biggest weaknesses is setting the time, right, rigidly and sticking to it, because there's always something in a residential unit [laughs] that makes you say 'Oh, I've gotta go and do this'.

The potential for practice development in supervision is shown clearly here, as is the likelihood that this important work may be de-prioritised in the face of more immediate concerns. As another manager shows, a preferred way of operating was by making the most of available opportunities to work alongside staff. In this way managers would become familiar with what was taking place in the home and also had potential to model practice:

> I prefer to work on the shop floor, obviously I prefer to be a manager that leads from the front and it is – others are learning from my example really. I prefer to be going down to the parents' evenings, I prefer to be in all the meetings and that's where I am. But I also recognise the weakness in that in the fact that, you know, I have to let go and let other people have those developmental opportunities – i.e. my assistant manager. That's how I prefer to work with the children, and very much the same with the staff, you know. My staff will tell you I know everything that's going on, I make it my business to find out everything that's going on. I'm very firm but I'm very fair – I mean, this is the way it's done but it's open for discussion and development. I believe I'm very professional and I like things to be done in a very professional way.

Nearly all managers volunteered that they would not ask staff to do tasks which they were not prepared to do themselves. Although most managers did not work in a hands-on capacity routinely themselves, working alongside staff was one way of providing practice examples and support. All managers preferred to observe what was taking place in their homes, rather than relying solely on communicating activities and areas of importance through formal means, such as handovers and supervision:

> I manage by walking about a lot… I don't do the shifts and I don't do the role of the senior care officer. I might, my hours might consist of coming up at ten o'clock and going home at eight so that I can see the practice on a night-time with the young people. I also see glimpses of practice during the day as well with, that's one part of managing by walking about, I can see glimpses when children are not at school how they intervene with young people and how they keep them engaged… I have tea at least twice a week at the home to get in touch with the young people and give them time and space to come up to my room if they want to talk about anything that's bothering them or if they want to talk about the adults, how they intervene, complaints if you like… [I'm also] looking at incident reports, looking at diary sheets, checking out, you know, looking at review reports, looking at all the systems we have in place and picking up if there's any development areas there with people in, in one-to-one, checking really.

Managers could only go so far with modelling practice. Nevertheless, it was often the case that managers *liked* to work shifts, as their hearts lay in providing direct child care and this provided an opportunity to assess staff skills and needs.

Often, acting in a hands-on capacity was thought of as a way of maintaining continuity for staff and young people, and obviated the need for agency staff. Agency staff were positively regarded only if they were known to the young people and the staff team, and even then only as a last resort. Their use was seen as indicative generally of crisis: one home recalled dealing with a protracted period of young people responding to loss through anger and aggression that left them using approximately 60 agency staff in a period of three months. Managers themselves preferred to provide cover rather than draw on agency staff:

> We use very, very few sessional staff here. We never have done, we use very few. You know, sometimes they're more of a hindrance than a help and we would just prefer to get on and do it ourselves and, you know, if we haven't got the ability [to] cover the shift then I cover it because, I don't know, it's not martyrdom, it's just that's what we think we should do and we have very few members of staff coming and going at the same consistent rate.

This was succinctly put by one manager as:

> I am the ultimate relief team!

Being available in this way provided a form of security for staff. Managers were aware, however, that their availability could tip over into interference in shifts if they did not guard against it, resulting in staff feeling undermined. Being on call, or available to provide advice by phone, was seen as a positive way to reassure staff. This was particularly important at times when staff were likely to feel most vulnerable, such as at evenings and weekends. Often such availability was felt to provide sufficient support and was not drawn upon frequently in the main by the majority of staff.

Being on call in this or other ways, however, did impact negatively on managers' personal lives. This was especially the case where the home was going through a difficult patch – for example, with unsettled behaviours around a new admission. Managers found ways to reduce the impact on their home lives, some by bringing the two spheres closer together, some by strict separation. In some organisations duty on call cover was provided; in other organisations managers came to some kind of informal agreement between themselves and their peers. Where others were consulted about occurrences in the home, considerable energy had to be devoted to communicating what had taken place and the like. Drawing on external resources, whether informal or formal, was regarded as somehow rocking the boat, and own activity was the preferred option. Most managers were happy to be available on call at any time, although of course there were times when this became burdensome.

Summary

This is the first of three chapters that focus on the process of managing children's homes. Building on previous work related to the tasks of residential staff (Whitaker *et al.* 1998), the chapter develops a detailed understanding of what takes place when staff teams and managers establish working relationships within the dynamic residential environment.

Creating, maintaining, influencing and in effect developing a staff team is a complex activity in and of itself. Where this occurs in a relationship-based environment such as a children's home, it is an essential preliminary to help the staff group to meet the needs of young people. It has to be addressed capably in order for work to take place. As reflected in other research about residential child care, relationship-forming is crucially important (Baldwin 1990; Berridge 2002). Management of staff teams working in children's homes involves much more than the administration of a bureaucratic system.

The nature of the post of manager clearly has an impact on the potential for purposeful work. The ways in which managers come into post, the status of their posts, changes in purpose and function of the home, and long periods of uncertainty about the direction of the home and/or the post itself are important individual factors. When these are less than positive experiences and are experienced simultaneously, they present fundamental challenges to the functioning of the home.

Accomplishing a functioning team entails drawing together individuals into a co-operating group such that they are able to share managers' clarity on goals and ways of achieving these. Managers are heavily involved in transmitting and determining the purpose of their homes, and in assisting their staff to realise that purpose. Part of this includes:

- delegating and sharing responsibilities to enable staff to see and play their own part in purposeful work
- developing the skills and confidence of staff
- finding effective ways of sustaining what staff do within a set of defined purposes.

Forming a coherent staff team requires sensitive work, which has to be revisited in response to changes in group composition, both staff and resident.

Building relationships with staff takes time for all concerned and staff skills and responses have to be individually assessed, especially where few records exist of experience and capabilities. The pace at which to introduce new approaches or changes in personnel has to be judged carefully. Making personnel changes capably has the potential to inspire confidence and trust in shaping the overall direction of the home.

Sharing roles and responsibilities relies on a solid understanding of the strengths of each member of staff and time spent both formally and informally in maintaining the staff team. A fundamental part of the manager's role involves achieving a balance between empowering staff and retaining decision-making authority. Crucially, managers and staff work together interdependently to establish a collaborative culture that is led and developed by the manager from within a hierarchical system of accountability.

Clearly, the tasks noted in this chapter require particular skills. Managers act as energisers, have presence, but not so much that staff are disempowered. They maintain buoyancy when things take a negative turn, offer practical alternatives when things get stuck, take responsibility but do not act hierarchically. They supervise, coach, educate, develop and enculture staff. They must be able to spend sufficient time within their homes to do all these things as well as top them up; they must act as supervisors, and as the person who checks and monitors. They use a collaborative approach that is fair, and which takes account of staff differences and is in turn reflected in the way staff work with young people. Managers adopt sufficient distance from their team to retain authority, maintain respect and be able to motivate when they are often the repository of negativity.

In sum, we have shown that in relation to staff teams managers have to find formal and informal ways to know and be confident in staff capabilities, such that they are able both to achieve identified goals on behalf of the young people and to maintain the staff group. These are ongoing activities.

In the next chapter we turn to an examination of the ways in which managers maintain their own specific roles within the context of their wider organisations.

Chapter 4

Shaping and Maintaining the Role of Manager within the Context of the Wider Organisation

Introduction

In Chapter 3 we showed the ways in which managers create, maintain and influence their staff teams. The present chapter goes on to explore what is entailed in sustaining the specific role of a manager, both individually and within the context of the parent organisation.

Clearly, the work arenas outlined so far require high levels of resilience and robust coping mechanisms on the part of managers themselves. What are the crucial self-management skills and supports that residential managers need to do their jobs well? Perhaps unsurprisingly, many of the attributes which managers hope to draw out of their staff members and the young people in their care are ones which they embody themselves. Key among these are being a confident practitioner, supervisor and manager, worthy of trust, who is capable of practising autonomously in a clearly defined goal-oriented manner. Vital aspects in shaping these characteristics are: managers' autonomy and freedom of discretion; supervision and support for managers; sharing responsibilities and feeling valued across the organisation; contributing to strategic management; spending time in the home itself; and opportunities for stimulation and development.

Managers' autonomy and freedom of discretion

Autonomy and the analysis of its role in respect of the effectiveness of organisations has a long history. Blau, for example, pointed to the necessity for functional autonomy in relation to smaller units within large organisations such that they have potential to organise in relation to their own needs (Blau 1964). The relative merits or negative consequences of autonomy has in turn long played a part in debates about residential child care environments. Research has indicated that feelings of autonomy are closely linked with clarity of purpose (Sinclair and Gibbs 1998a). This latter has been shown consistently as important to the effectiveness of homes (Berridge and Brodie 1998; Brown *et al.* 1998; Sinclair and Gibbs 1998a). Being in control of the home and able to manage things in their own distinctive way was seen by managers in our research as both vital and motivating, contributing to a sense of achievement in relation to the young people.

The extent to which managers felt themselves to have full autonomy – i.e. the 'right' to make decisions on how work was carried out, tasks allocated, shared and rota-ed without involving senior managers – was largely dependent on the manager's dynamic relationship with their own organisation, established over time:

> As a manager what I like is the fact that I'm allowed to make decisions and I have control over my unit, and I'm not directed in the sense that, y'know, directed to take children in or to work in a particular way and I think that's what works extremely well for me, and I tend to give that same opportunity to my staff.

In this way, being able to work autonomously was seen as highly rewarding, giving a sense of purpose and value to the task of children's home manager while allowing sufficient scope for flexibility and creativity. Autonomy was not assumed as a given, rather it was a matter of reciprocal exchange between the manager and the parent organisation:

> At the end of the day I have credibility, I don't tend to go off on one about insignificant issues, you know. I don't tend to stamp my feet, I quietly get on with doing the job that I'm paid to do, that I do as well as I can do and, to provide a good service for people and I think my reputation allows that kind of autonomy, does that make sense? ... I've always believed that if I work hard, all right, I'll do OK, the clients will get a good deal out of me and the organisation does well because they've got somebody who's prepared to work hard. The organisation responds by saying 'He works hard so actually perhaps he does know what he's talking about

occasionally, and it doesn't mean he's always going to be right and it doesn't mean we've always got to pay any attention but we have to extend that back to him', and that's how I feel they treat me.

Feeling autonomous was seen to rely on effective communication within the organisation, where managers were empowered and at the same time had established channels for information-sharing which enabled progress to be noted throughout the hierarchy:

> I've never been brought to account on anything that I've done but I do have regular meetings with her [my supervisor] and we have business progress meetings every month, we have managers' meetings every month, so there's every opportunity for people to bring things to the table that they're concerned about, whether it be from staff below me, as it were, making comments in staff meetings, to the directors and so on at business progress meetings.

Another manager described the degrees of freedom around her task in the following way:

> Obviously the way I practise is guided by the things they ask me to do and by the [organisation's] residential strategy, etc. So in that sense, so long as I'm paying attention to what they're asking me to do, I do that in my own way and I'm not directed.

Autonomy was largely seen as being afforded subject to having proved oneself in terms of experience and reputation, fitting in with the organisation itself, being respected and usually liked by senior managers, being seen as obliging, dependable and non-threatening. Personality clashes and over-assertive approaches made this fit unlikely.

Some organisations were structured so that the manager's autonomy was reduced by dint of hierarchical division of roles across management tiers. One organisation shared roles and responsibilities for their homes across three management tiers. Another was moving from close control of managers of homes by reference to regulation and company guidelines, together with high levels of involvement of their line manager, towards a more devolved responsibility, in line with perceptions of new national standards for residential managers.

As noted previously, and perhaps somewhat surprisingly given the gravity of the task, most immediate autonomy was felt as afforded where the brief was charged with high levels of responsibility – for example, where a manager appointed as temporary was assigned to the home in order to redeem it. In such circumstances high levels of confidence were required on the part of the manager:

> I think I was given very much a free hand to do whatever really. I suppose I felt well in control of the destiny of the home really and they [the organisation] would support me one way or the other and I think that made me feel I wasn't under [pressure]. I think it was thought that nobody could do it and it would fail so I could only win really, you know what I mean? I think if I'd have come out of it and said 'No, I think it needs to close and we need to start again' they'd have accepted that quite happily. But I didn't think that was fair on some of the people that, you know, because I think when you start breaking things completely you've got to start mending them completely and I think it was a hell of a struggle.

At this point, we must draw attention to the distinction between autonomy, which entails active ownership of task in hand, and being able to act in isolation with little direction, whether at the level of initial appointment or further down the line. Where this latter kind of situation was encountered, managers were forced into proactivity in engaging their line managers, albeit usually with some attendant understanding rationale which took into account the demanding nature of the line manager's role. In the following account of a negative experience, the manager felt that the footing on which he had started life in the home had not yet been transcended, and his feelings of being isolated within the wider organisation had increased over time:

> On the one hand I do like the autonomy, I don't want somebody breathing down my back all the time. On the other hand I think it's especially important to anybody, irrespective of post, when you come into a new job that, you know, you have some direction and some kind of a welcome. Because I mean if you sort of take it a step further I mean I'm sure my feelings for the children and young people that come into the home were increased in terms of empathy because if you think what it's like for a young person to come into a children's home not knowing anybody, not knowing where everything is, etc., etc., it's very similar really. It's quite interesting.

Although the majority of managers encountered difficulties in communicating with line managers from time to time, almost all regarded themselves as responsible for easing the relationship and bringing it to good standing by communicating the residential task where necessary, or by emphasising what they needed at a particular moment. Managers' sense of being able to act to influence the form and meaning of the relationship was keenly held – that is to say, their sense of their own agency (and capacity) in this respect was high.

In terms of resources, particularly staffing, the manager's flexibility was shaped by external influence and control. Increases in staff hours were always controlled from outside the home in some fashion, with the extent of freedom of discretion being defined at organisational level beyond which managers had to seek permission for overuse. Exceptions usually related to homes in crisis, where increases in staffing ratios were approved without question according to the perceived difficulty of the task.

A particular and recurrent problem in the week-by-week running of homes was the use of staff time off in lieu (TOIL), which often amassed to such an extent that it became impossible to take time off which corresponded to the numbers of hours owed without producing further displacement of staff hours. This local negotiation of additional resourcing would at times get out of hand for managers, producing disharmony among the staff group, which in turn increased stressors within the home. Ultimately, where no apparently fair agreement could be reached about time owed, staff would take sick leave in order to retrieve and make recompense for time given in goodwill. This kind of strained spiralling could only be contained locally for a limited period, and once drawn to the attention of senior managers would become evidence of poor functioning. In some situations, managers were able to build a case for additional permanent staffing thereby reducing unpredictable increases in staff time, but these situations rarely came to fruition. Somewhat ironically, cases were most likely to be successful if practice was deemed good and outcomes judged by the organisation as consistently positive.

The ways that rotas were drawn up and allocated depended on the structure of the organisation. Where organisations and homes were small, rotas were often written and allocated centrally. Smaller homes usually worked with a consistently high ratio of staff to young people come what may. In larger organisations, the structuring of rotas and the allocation of staff was a matter for individual homes to manage. In the latter case, it was both necessary and possible to vary staff time according to the daily needs of young people as individuals and as a group.

Supervision and support for managers from their parent organisations

Support for managers from their parent organisations was provided in some way for all, with opportunities given both formally and informally. The frequency and type of support varied according to managers' formal and informal status within the organisation, the climate of the home, the extent to which managers felt the need for support, or thought it appropriate to draw upon, and perceptions of the line manager's approach to their job.

Frequent overseeing of the way the home was progressing overall was reported across the sample. This often took the form of group meetings, where managers and those directly responsible for them came together to discuss new developments in terms of policies and procedures, and, in some cases, to discuss more generally progress within individual homes.

The frequency of occurrence of more detailed supervision and personal development work varied considerably. The most usually reported situation was that individual support from and contact with external managers was on an 'as and when necessary' basis, which was often preferred by the children's home manager. Many experienced high levels of willingness to offer support without concomitant capacity to provide it:

> I have to say that my line manager's very approachable so if, if I did have any kind of problem or issue, you know, I can phone him, even at home, he's not averse to that. I just think his time is so tied up now that he can't manage to get around his managers in the way that he did when the service was initially set up.

A few experienced supervision as a somewhat one-sided opportunity for their line managers to give their views on performance:

> I've had one supervision since I've been back [from secondment] which was literally three hours of her speaking, saying to me this, this, this. I'm not exaggerating, twelve things emerged three hours later and it's like, you're sat in a meeting and it's like 'Well this was supposed to be done yesterday'. 'Well actually I've just come back and you said...' and thank goodness I recorded some of this stuff. So it's, it's quite a lot of pressure from external to the home right now on me, and again my staff team, it has been a very difficult, and as they describe it, an unsupportive time while I've been away, so I can't automatically start delegating, I need time to sort of boost their morale and sort of lift the spirits in the home before I'm going to get any sort of, you know, efficient, effective kind of work out of them, if you see what I mean?

Supervision was seen as most legitimately utilised in times of crisis. Often regular supervision and support was forgone if the home was ticking over well or line managers were seen to be exceedingly busy. Often confirming what a manager had done by reporting back to their line manager was labelled as supervision by both parties. The way in which support was provided varied, for example, by formal appointments, by phone as and when needed, unplanned visits to the home, email exchanges and contact by mail.

Sometimes it was a matter of personal pride not to draw on external support, while in other cases managers felt it essential to their practice to be supervised. This usually depended on the nature of the relationship between the residential manager and their external manager. Where trust and mutual respect were present, supervision was thought of as valuable in whatever form it took. Style and approach to supervision was seen to vary across the sample and for individual managers over time, as shown in the following example, which is a researcher's synopsis of a long narrative piece:

> I didn't want her there, physically, but just on some days I thought, sod this, and then I needed her, she'd been my line manager for two years, and when I did need her it was a blue light flashing, she was there, she cancelled meetings and prioritised what I needed. She rang me twice a week, and I would ring her. Her telephone advice kept me going, and made me feel very secure. She's now moved on and I've now got another service manager. We have a completely different relationship, and I've got to accept that. For support, I've never found a concrete formula, I meet up with other managers at managers' meetings, otherwise I'm quite insular, and it seems now that we've got a vast amount of service managers, who have different approaches, and it now seems that what I took for granted as being an organisational stance from my previous line manager may have been more of a personal take on what was required at organisational level. It seems to be about personalities. For example, two managers did something very similar with a young person and one was told off and the other was given approval and supported. I used to have a lot of confidence in my previous manager as what she said was what was supposed to be done. [Researcher's synopsis]

Managers' confidence in the reliability, consistency and authority of the support provided was crucial. The spirit of not really needing constant or regular supervision per se, rather needing more of an advocate than a supervisor, was typical in the majority of homes:

> This [person] who's my supervisor, I've known her for a long time, she's worked in the department as long as I have, very nice [person] and very supportive, her style I struggle with. So basically [coughing] sorry, I've had to say to her 'Please don't pat me on the head all the time, I cannot cope with that. Please don't tell me how wonderful I am, that's not what I need to hear. What I need to know is when it, when the shit hits the fan

basically you're gonna go to bat for me, that you're gonna protect this service.'

And the value of line managers as corroborators of practice was frequently avowed:

> She's quite an empowering style of [line] manager, she does a lot of listening and a lot of suggesting and because I'm developing, I'm quite a developed person myself now, I can say that with confidence, that I don't abuse that and I stick within the, I stay within the aims of the department, the objectives and the philosophy and the values of the department. That is my guide. As long as I'm working within their philosophy and their, their, their style and I feel as though they're quite confident to make decisions. And I always feedback and check out with my line manager whether, whether I'm doing OK, whether that's OK, especially when I make mistakes and it's usually with people that I'm indeed leading.

Experiencing continuity by sharing information, particularly in respect of progress within the home, was thought to be valuable. The following manager also shows that supervision was experienced as being about practice as distinct from being developmental, as was often the case throughout the sample:

> I get regular supervision, [although] it's quite different in lots of ways to supervision. I mean when I had supervision with [line manager's name], we did obviously talk about all of, practice issues, work related stuff, but I would also talk to her about its impact on me, whereas I don't tend to do that with my [line] manager…but because of the regular supervision she obviously is up to speed with everything that's going on in the unit and I probably speak to her outside of supervision several times a week anyway and quite often she will be on the strategy groups or working groups as well. So there is a lot of communication and compared to how we were managed up to about two and a half years ago it's really very good and it's quite supportive.

It was very clearly the case that most residential managers had firm ideas about what they needed from supervision, and set out to achieve this for themselves. Where their aims became impossible to achieve, they most often took this as indicative of personal failing, or as evidence of structural barriers, where, for example, organisational size meant that relationships became distant.

Above all, the line manager/residential manager relationship was valued to check out performance and retain a boundary around pressures which were discharged within the home, thereby reducing strains on staff in the home and providing a safety valve for the manager of the home:

> I also like to have feedback from my line manager and just really as you would, it can be quite isolating because we don't, you don't have a peer group, you know. Like the seniors have each other and their care officers on shift I just have me really and I can't rely on seniors to give me that feedback all the time and it puts them in an awkward position sometimes. Sometimes they feel they can't or sometimes they feel they, I'm trying to encourage them to actually give me that, the feedback, whether that's room for improvement for me or, or good feedback, say 'Oh you did that really well'. I am trying to increase that but there's some things that, that require line management feedback and checking out really. So I do rely on it as a support and it's an appropriate support because in the past, because I haven't had that, I've sought that support from seniors and that hasn't been healthy.

The corroborative power of the formally identified line manager was a major source of reaffirmation and reassurance.

Support from other sources

In addition to support and supervision provided by line managers, opportunities to exchange views with groups of peers and colleagues from other arms of provision within managers' wider organisations were sought and were highly valued:

> As a group of managers we get together on a monthly basis with our line manager and we look at development issues, legislative issues and matters that perhaps have arisen within the organisation and we, we discuss them, you know, and then quite often we're given individual responsibilities for areas of development and we'll take that back and then bring it back too. So I think as a group of managers there is support there and support for each other and, you know, the support to develop and share particular items that you want to progress within the unit in relation to, to obviously legislation and everything else that's going on.

Other forms of support were found at an individual level – for example, from family or friends:

> I don't need my residential managers very much at all. [Pause] I'm not a person who particularly has [pause], it's a sad reflection on myself, who has a great deal of sort of friends really, and after I've barked at you for the last half hour you're probably not surprised. I'm a great listener! I'm not

actually, that's a poor bit of me, so I don't use the residential management group very much. I use my [pause] I use my partner I suppose who, he works in the same sort of work.

And from other managers individually, by means of advice and encouragement:

I went through a time in early summer when I, I got another manager over and I said 'Look, what the hell am I doing wrong? Cos it's just, I'm just not winning, you know, I'm not getting it, I don't seem to be making any headway' and he said 'No, I think you're doing everything you can'…Of course everybody was getting jumpy cos this other person and all he did was just come down and be another pair of eyes for me really and, you know, he said 'No, I think you're doing exactly what you should be doing and if you continue hopefully it'll turn.'

And through other professional channels:

I do have my own personal therapy which, which is where I take that [pressure-laden] sort of thing but it's, I would say that the relationship is very different and, there are also quite a lot of things that go on in, not in, not with the children so much but in the staff team that if you shared all of it, all of the time [pause] it would cause, it would cause more problems, if you like. So it's easier to hold it myself really.

Clearly, it was important not to be left alone with a difficult situation for which trusted advice and/or support was thought to be necessary. It was also important not to overuse the availability of line managers, or to use their support as a first resort rather than relying on one's own resources:

I suppose in, in many ways the only time I've had to really ring her out of, out of sort of our formal supervision is, I suppose whenever I've had to finally say 'Look, we can't continue to look after this young person, it's too damaging to x, y, z' then that's the time I've, I've had to telephone her and ask for that sort of advice or assistance… I certainly wouldn't go to her without having either tried every option or…you know, gone down every avenue or gone to, you know, the farthest end really, I certainly wouldn't go to her unprepared and I think she sort of appreciates that.

In sum, residential managers felt themselves to need sufficient freedom to 'get on with the job' while having access to support in decision making if they should feel they needed it. What they valued most was an 'on demand' accessible and trustworthy reference point at senior level in the organisational hierarchy.

Sharing responsibilities and feeling valued across the organisation

Some managers felt that they were working within an organisational context which promoted collective responsibility, where procedures were universal and all staff would be familiar with daily routines and expectations within each of the homes, and, furthermore, where senior staff throughout the members of the hierarchy were approachable:

> I think the thing I like working at [this home] [for] is it, to some degree rewards hard work. If you're committed and you're part of the team and you work to one goal, you get a satisfaction out of that as well. I think it's rewarded by the organisation as I said and the other thing is, is if I become unhappy I can knock the director's door and let her know I'm unhappy and I can talk to her. I can talk to the proprietor, whether that's, you know, I can ring her up on a Saturday night and say 'Y, I'm just feeling a bit like this' or 'I'm a bit concerned about this' and I try not to do it because everybody's weekend's important but if I needed to do that I can do it, and when I'm on call at a weekend I'm not left, excuse the pun, holding the baby, you know. If I've got a very, very contentious difficult awkward situation and I'm not sure that what I'm doing is probably the right thing or if I think it is the right thing but I just need some confidence, I can ring A, I can ring B, I can ring Y and people will gladly accept my call. It's not a chore, it's a global acceptance of what we do.

Being valued by a group of senior managers and integrated into the organisation as a whole was felt as valuable as affording respect to managers of homes. Feeling engaged with the wider service helped to shape direction for managers:

> [My manager says] 'We think, we think that you do a good job.' I mean our SSI [Social Services Inspectorate] and joint review inspections that we had last year came out very, very well for looked after. We got a lot of input and a lot of briefing about those inspections prior to them happening but then we also got very clear feedback about what we needed, what we did well but also what we needed to develop as well. We kept informed through team briefing which is, is [pause] as our manager says, you know, if you don't know anything it's not because you haven't been told, it's because you haven't been listening, and we get everything coming through on a month-to-month basis. So sort of locally on our sort of, on our children's service brief but also the bigger picture, the bigger sort of, the core brief, the social services brief and all the stuff that's happening with health at the moment, for example, and all the Quality Protects stuff

that we're kept informed about. So you get a firm feeling of where you are within the bigger picture, that's been a big help for, for us all I think, this sort of information given in team briefings.

Where feelings of injustice in relation to one's own position were apparent, these acted as constraining blocks to practice and grievances accumulated that had negative consequences. Where the kinds of fairness that managers extended to their staff were not in evidence for themselves, managers' motivation was difficult to sustain. Feeling secure in one's place within the wider organisation and with relationships within the hierarchy was regarded as a great enabler. Being in contact directly with members of senior management was also important:

I like the management structure we've got now, it's the best one we've got since I've been here because it's clear and it's direct, you know. You get credits for the stuff that you do and, which I'm pleased about, but you also know that if there's something that you haven't, you know, you get told about the cock-ups that you've made which I'm also fine about that. Whether, I mean my assistant director, I've got a, I'm managed by a team manager then there is a divisional manager on, next one up, then there's the assistant director and the director. So I come into contact with all of them. The director and the assistant director have visited here in the last six months, I'm in regular contact with my manager and I know that my divisional manager's easily accessible. If I, if they ask me to do some stuff I will send it to them and I'll say, you know, 'Will you be absolutely critical about what I'm doing because, you know, I need your feedback on, on how I've done'. For example, if I'm writing a piece of guidance…

Being held in high regard with proper recognition throughout the organisation was felt to be reaffirming and to legitimise managers' access to further professional development:

So I suppose what I'm trying to say in a nutshell is…[my home]…is what I work from, it's the base I work from and that's where you see reputation comes from really within your management role, that people see your management skills, they see the success that you make of what you're managing and that sort of impinges on the wider organisation in the fact that, you know, I'm given opportunities to move into other areas.

Clearly, the feeling of being valued could outweigh other perceived injustices, and help towards sustaining motivation:

I don't feel as if I'm paid enough but I feel as if I'm valued for what I do and, you know, and whether that's just, I suppose that is what good management's about I suppose, it's about getting the most out of people and paying them as little as possible [laughter]!

Building a creditable reputation within the organisation was seen as empowering in itself, both in terms of managing the home and being given permission to develop oneself by taking on interests outside the home. These included aspects of policy or procedural planning in conjunction with senior managers, acting as manager at another home, or serving as substitutes for senior managers at external functions. Acting at quasi-policy level was seen both as beneficial to managers themselves and as a distraction from directly managing the home.

Contributing to strategic management

Many managers were expected by their organisation to work on tasks not directly related to the home. There was a general ambivalence about being involved more widely in strategic management arenas, an oft-reported situation. Where homes were relatively settled, managers were more likely to regard taking part in other activities on behalf of the organisation as beneficial. For some the overriding feeling was that 'it seems to be more and more that we're dragged away from the house'. At times this was in relation to strategic work within the parent organisation:

> You're more removed from the team and the young people and very much more reliant upon the senior residential workers and if you've got good ones, that's great, if you've got those, you know, that you can depend on to be making sure things are happening as they should be happening day by day but sometimes that's not always the case... There's been an awful lot of working groups, strategy groups, that, where managers have had to sort of come together off unit and work with, on the minimum standards to see, you know, where our gaps are and how we go about sort of, you know, putting things right, so, that's impacted on the unit a great deal cos I'm hardly ever at the unit.

This was regarded as a double-edged challenge, requiring additional energy while being stimulating and beneficial:

> I guess because we, we're dealing sort of first hand with lots of other agencies now, you know, working in partnership, and because of all the new standards and whatever, people are having to be out there a lot more and network and, you know, so I think we will, we were all expecting the change although it has been, I mean as annoying as it is because it takes

you away from what you need to be doing it's also, you know, it's also enlightening and you do, you do learn a lot from it.

Such a challenge represented a major shift over time in the way managers of homes were expected to work, with inputs required at strategic levels in terms of Best Value initiatives, Quality Protects and the like. While some managers felt able to become fully involved in relationships across the boundary of the home in this way, others felt that they had not been well prepared in advance for this:

> I thought I was fairly clear about the expectations of the job in terms of job description; obviously the further I got in post I didn't realise that it, that they expect you to be head of the children's home but they also expect you to be a manager of sort of at a strategic, outside of the home level and probably as time goes on I feel like it's – the balance has tipped more towards the outside management stuff which all, not all of it but most of it does have some indirect relevance to the impact of the children and their care at the home but, you know, it's a great leap to make that. There's, to me there's not enough time spent on the task at the home and they expect you to sort of spread yourself out until you're so thin, that wasn't very clear. On the other hand, on a positive note, I mean it's, some of the experiences have been good in terms of my own professional development, I've been able to develop different areas which will be beneficial in my next post, if you see what I mean?

The impact of this kind of work in addition to working with the staff team often left managers feeling as though they had insufficient space to perform home-based work well:

> But in terms of, I thought I would be more a sort of a children's home manager, leader of the team, you know…guide, steer, direct, motivate that staff team, not do that, which is a big enough job in itself, plus everything else and…that's the way things are but I feel I manage to delegate too much anyway.

Managers were keen to have input into the direction of their parent organisations; however, a balance had to be established in relation to day-to-day work in the home itself.

Spending time in the home itself

Strategic external work was at times perceived as taking managers away from being able to sustain the close in-practice relationships they felt necessary to maintain in order to manage their homes successfully.

Overall, the amount of time managers were able to spend within their homes varied according to the climate of the home at given points, the formal or informal status of the manager within the wider organisation, organisational expectations and requirements, and the individual needs of the manager.

High proportions of time spent in the home were considered across the sample to enable positive conditions for work for the manager and staff alike. All managers intended to be closely in contact with their homes. Many managers felt themselves unable to spend sufficient time within their homes; this was largely due to circumstances beyond their control. Managers preferred to know and understand the dynamics of tasks and relationships as they existed in their homes – that is to say, what work was taking place and how it was occurring. Actually playing a part in this, or being able to observe practice, was thought to be a vital and irreplaceable part of the manager's task. Oral or written communication about what was taking place was thought of as supporting, rather than substituting for, managers' direct assessments of interpersonal relationships and practice.

For homes in crisis or with particular difficulties to address, it was most usually the case that managers felt they were expected by the organisation to spend the majority of their work time within the unit. Further to this, managers felt compelled to spend time in the unit if things were going badly, usually in order to help get things back on course by means of educating, coaching or role-modelling for staff in some fashion. Where managers had spent considerable periods away from the home, they often reverted to working shifts for a limited time in order to recover their 'finger on the pulse'.

Extended periods of absence were regarded by managers as meriting some form of compensating activity, such as an increase in usual time spent in the home, using a more 'hands-on' approach for a time-limited period, doing more 'sleep-in' duties than would usually be the case, or just generally being available by 'popping in' to the home to keep company with young people and staff. Some managers were able to do these things alongside periods of absence by making use of their own time. Others were unable to do so due to domestic commitments. For many, 'topping-up' contact with the home was curtailed according to personal circumstances, and many managers experienced regret when changes in personal life occurred – for example, when providing care for relatives or having a baby prevented this. This participative shortcut to achieving familiarity with what was taking place, however, was seen to risk being able to retain sufficient distance from practice to assess the overall situation of the home.

Most managers made a point of routinely spending time in the home outside office hours, usually after school or at meal times with the young people. In effect, although it was seen as a vital part of the task, this form of contact in many cases occurred during the manager's own time, as nine to five demands were already high. Paperwork was often completed at home, and accumulated TOIL brought its own attendant difficulties. In such cases, it was seen as simpler to pay attention to the home during 'own time', and in that way the pace of creating and maintaining relationships was unforced by other concerns.

Opportunities for stimulation and development

Pursuing external interests linked to the home was seen by many managers as an important way of retaining buoyancy and stimulation. Sometimes this came in the form of extending the range of work carried out in the home, sometimes developing own skills, and sometimes by accepting the challenge of managing a further unit:

> I'm going to be very careful how I say this, depending on who you're saying it to, that maybe once I've got stuff up and running and it's being managed that I become bored, that may be a major concern for me, that I'm, [this home] runs extremely well, it's got an extremely good reputation within [the organisation]…and now I've, I've set that all up, etc., I may become bored and thinking, well I need another task. And maybe that's why they gave me another unit. I don't know. But I mean I think for me that's, that's the difficulty that presents for me.

Once established and feeling confident and secure in their positions, some managers looked to stimulation for themselves by taking on other activities – for example, family assessment work for fostering placements, fostering panels, on-call for family placements, or reviewing of some kind. This added to workloads in so far as these managers developed extensive networks and responsibilities outside their homes. Managers overall were very well able to contend with challenges; indeed, many thrived on these and, when homes were stable and smooth running over long periods of time, some would feel compelled to look for personal development in the form of external opportunities. In such cases, additional, self-imposed tasks were seen as vital to keeping these managers buoyant and in touch with developments beyond the apparent confines of the home itself:

> I get twitchy when I feel that I'm just sort of confined to this little house in [place name], it's part of a huge sort of service. So I've looked outside to think, well it's all about me broadening my role but also making people, I suppose I'm ambitious to a certain extent I suppose and it's about doing more interesting things and proving to other people that you can be creative and that you can take part more in policy and to be a little bit sort of more strategic as far as taking part in things that affect all our homes... There's lots and lots of stuff I do outside of, outside of [this home] which, though it brings added pressure to what I have to do here because it limits you on time, it keeps me going. It's about how I manage that I suppose and it, it gives me what I want and it also keeps me motivated within my work-place to do the other stuff that probably I would find a little bit mundane after sort of six years. Not mundane – but you need extra challenges. I feel as if I'm well-managed.

A frequently expressed view was that there were very few development opportunities for managers of homes. A move to more senior management positions, where interpersonal and educative skills would be very differently employed, would mean that experience with young people would not be a direct priority and was therefore regarded as negative.

Summary

This is the second of three chapters focusing on the process of managing children's homes. The chapter provides an understanding of what is needed to sustain the specific role of manager at both the level of the individual and that of the parent organisation, and what influences the degrees of autonomy afforded to managers. In doing so, the chapter adds to previous work about managers' roles and their relationships with external managers (Sinclair and Gibbs 1998a; Whipp *et al.* 2005; Whitaker *et al.* 1998).

Throughout this current chapter we have reflected the self-management skills and supports which residential managers in our sample felt themselves to need to do their jobs well. As individuals, managers have the potential for attaining high levels of influence over their staff teams and the young people in their care. In order to create and sustain confidence in their own performance, they are reliant on establishing credibility within their own organisations while needing to feel that they have sufficient control over their own homes to practise flexibly and with an appropriate degree of autonomy.

At the same time, managers need to have a sense that they are not left on their own with a problem, have line-management support and supervision when needed, and have access to sufficient development opportunities. They need to feel as though they are being treated fairly and with a respect equal to that of their peers, and that they are valued by their parent organisation. Managers value a close relationship with and access to their organisational hierarchy. They also value being involved in strategic management, contributing to the planning process for their homes, and assisting in writing and developing procedures across their parent organisations. In addition, managers need to have access to external opportunities in order to develop themselves professionally, retain buoyancy and uphold a sense of progression and stimulation.

In sum, this chapter has shown that managers must fulfil organisational requirements and learn how to use their own support systems to best effect, even when these are somewhat lacking. They must be confident and clear in approach with their own organisations. They must know when and how to seek support, and be capable of sharing responsibilities across the organisation. At the same time they must be able to spend sufficient time within their homes to sustain their teams directly and keep in close contact with the functioning of their homes.

We turn next to the key task in hand for children's homes, that of working in relation to the needs of young people. The next chapter builds on points raised in Chapters 3 and 4 and focuses on preferred ways of working with young people and how these are determined and influenced by managers and their teams.

Chapter 5

Shaping Work with Young People

Introduction

In the previous two chapters we saw something of the ways that managers of children's homes coach, educate, enculture and supervise staff as part of a continuing and evolving process, and what is entailed in sustaining the role of children's homes manager. The present chapter focuses on describing aspects of practice with young people and common *approaches* which managers are able to bring about in their homes. Elements of these include knowing young people's needs and characteristics, establishing boundaries and routines, building relationships, establishing keyworker systems, and developing and maintaining relationships with others such as field social workers and schools. We give examples from practice with young people in so far as they illustrate the approach being used, as distinct from focusing on all aspects of the work taking place.

The positive approaches described by managers in relation to their staff teams were often consciously intended to translate into preferred ways of practising with young people – for example, collaborative approaches, taking account of differences, being seen to be fair. The task for managers and staff alike was to bring about such approaches in direct, day-to-day work, in a manner that was consistent across the group of staff and young people, while respecting and focusing on individual needs. To achieve this successfully was a particularly complex, dynamic challenge.

To state the obvious, all young people resident in children's homes have already experienced complex lives. Most have experienced emotional strain and distress, many have experienced considerable changes in living situation including while being looked after, none are from backgrounds which render social, emotional or economic achievement easy. Some manifest high levels of distress in the form of disturbed or troubled behaviour. Individual young people's needs and those of the group are complex.

The balance between dealing with individual and group needs involved notions of parity and fairness, negotiation and juggling of resources. Some methods of working clearly focused on individuals – for example, keyworker systems. All methods were responsive to shifts in the dynamics of the home.

As shown by previous research, the range of characteristics which staff working in children's homes encounter includes chaotic behaviours, fearfulness, a sense of being lost, offending behaviours, inappropriate sexual behaviours and complex relationships with parents. Some combinations of contrasting needs present staff with few difficulties and many opportunities; others present few opportunities and many difficulties (Whitaker *et al.* 1998). Establishing thresholds for 'acceptable' behaviour from within this context is clearly a complex challenge (Barter *et al.* 2004). The ways that homes manage their task of caring for groups of young people within a context of changing needs is dynamically related to shifts in the equilibrium of the home, which may take considerable time to turn around.

Chapter 3 showed that the way that managers approach guiding direct work with young people is determined by many factors, not least being the staff team's ability to work together in a clear and consistent manner. All managers of the homes in our sample modelled practice in some form. The degree to which this was a 'talking' or 'hands-on' approach varied according to personal style, demands on time, the extent to which staff were afforded autonomy in practice, organisational structure and expectations, and the manager's perception of what the home needed at any given moment.

Knowing young people's needs and characteristics

A most usual starting point, as was seen in terms of working with the group of staff, was to identify young people's individual needs. This was seen as high priority at the point of admission to the home. To facilitate good practice, all managers were keen only to admit young people whom they regarded as matching the purpose and function of their unit, the skills of members of staff, and the tenor of the current resident group:

> I wouldn't take a child in if he wouldn't meet the criteria of the unit and I didn't believe that we had staff who were skilled to work with him. With a child who's got a major drug problem or a child who's got very offending

behaviour and it could have a traumatic effect on the other children, I have total control over who I admit into that unit and I've never, in all my time at [this organisation], had any manager say that I've had to admit a child. I've never been in that situation. That's the situation I was in in [my previous organisation] and that's what led me to leave, because you were consistently running, working in a crisis manner and I don't believe that's good for any unit. So I'm very, very fortunate that I've not been asked to take a child which I wouldn't, which I didn't feel would fit the unit.

In recent years the idea of getting the 'right mix' of young people in children's homes has come to be regarded as having greater priority than the 'heads-for-beds' solution to placement needs (Department of Health 1998). The most frequent challenge to the purpose and function of the home was in the form of pressure to accept admissions of young people who did not fall within the agreed remit for the home. In our two previous studies, dealing with the so-called 'heads-for-beds' approach of external managers, field social workers and placement officers was seen as a highly problematic area of practice. Considerable progress had occurred in most organisations in our present sample in respect of the 'appropriateness' of placements, and creative ways of working to bring about the best possible placements for young people were being prioritised. It was frequently the case that groups of residential managers within the organisation were involved in discussions with other relevant professionals about placements, and many thought that the requirements associated with the registration of residential managers would prove to be likely facilitators of greater control over who would come to live in the home and when.

Major difficulties still emerged, however. Although many positive procedural changes in the arena of admissions had taken place, level of control over admissions and thereby control over the purpose and function of the home was not within the gift of all managers in our sample. Responsibility for admissions was held at differing levels of the organisation, with greatest pressures to admit experienced directly by particular managers working within the local authority sector. In some large organisations placement panels that included residential managers had been established, and these were able to work in a planned way, taking account of the mix of young people currently placed in each home alongside the needs of the young person under discussion. Such provision was viewed positively by managers, but was not beyond being flouted on occasions. Other organisations agreed placements prior to the case being passed on to a manager, who then was able to agree or not to the young person coming to live in the home. The extent to which the manager felt able to 'hold out' against the requested placement varied considerably, often in line with the manager's standing within the organisation overall, but most usually in terms of the length of time a bed had been vacant and the prospect of a further young person seen on the horizon. Other organisations held responsibility for placement at senior management level and, although teams within homes were consulted, decisions as to placement were taken outside the home. This was found most clearly in those organisations where levels of responsibility across the organisation were tightly connected in terms of communication, and activity within the home was procedure driven, and supported and advised by senior managers on a day-to-day basis.

In the illustration of a new placement given next, the immediate impact of a lack of control over admissions on the resident group of young people forms part of the example:

> Well, you get consulted as to, you know, this youngster's around or these are around but at the end of the day the line managers would have their say. I mean I've got emergency placement overnight this morning and obviously, we didn't have any say in it, you know, there was a bed kind of there, that 'You've got a spare bed, so you will take him'... I walked in, you know, we're trying to get the kids to school this morning and their behaviour's slightly different this morning, you know. Two haven't gone this morning. You know, everybody can come out with some kind of argument to debate an issue through, but they may have thought, well who's this youngster coming this morning, who is he, we want to know more about him. He may have made them feel uncomfortable, you know. He hasn't gone to school so why should we go too, that kind of, you know. And so it's like something out the blue this morning, there's somebody in somebody's bed this morning, just a bit of information on him and that's it.

Sometimes young people were shunted about between placements without regard for effect on the individual or the group and against the will of the manager of the home. The value of a good start in relation to other young people at the point of entry into the home was not to be underestimated:

> Attempts had been made to sustain this temporary foster placement that he was in but that broke down but yesterday we had a situation where this young boy was actually sitting in the area team office, this is late afternoon, we'd all been in the managers' meeting yesterday afternoon, I was informed that we'd probably have to take this boy in, but the social worker actually brought, despite me asking him not to, brought the boy over and with all his belongings before I'd even had the opportunity to get over here and speak to the 16-year-old girl, you know. So we had to move her

out to another, a bed in another home and that, that caused a lot of upset because our existing residents felt highly indignant and aggrieved, you know, that Jo had been made to move like this. And so instead of being able to have Mark come in on a planned basis, you know, we have him come in and there's all sorts of mutterings and grumblings, you know, from, from the other residents about, you know, 'Well, that's not fair, he's taken Jo's bed', you know, and he got quite a rough ride, and it's not really good enough that is it?

Sometimes the level of apparent choice at the point of admission extended also to the young people themselves, and made for an even better fit within the resident group:

We've tightened up the referral, making sure we're getting the matching process right... The expectations are explained in some length to them [young people]. So nobody comes in, if you like, completely blind. I think that's different to a lot of children's homes around [here] where young people are moved from home to home or area to area, they don't get any choice in terms of how they live and where they live. Decisions are made for them. [Here] decisions are not made for them, it's their choice for them to come into [this kind of home] and not the other way around.

Once a placement had been made, part of identifying needs involved assessing risk areas for the young person and minimising opportunities for these to materialise:

[It's about] ensuring that there's tight supervision around really. And knowing your child and ensuring that your staff know your child, which is why we regularly discuss children at a staff meeting and having risk assessments in place. If you've got a child who, I mean just to describe some of the children we've had, who will find a knife and will pull a knife on a member of staff and we've had a number of those. The children who are willing to thrash out, kick staff, thump them in the face, because they've witnessed it within their own home. And you ensure that knives are locked away, you ensure that staff aren't leaving knives around, so that isn't an act available to a child, to take a knife and hurt a member of staff. It's that closing down areas for them which can, can cause some problems.

The care plan and its conversion into a residential plan was regarded as pivotal for the individual young person. At a practice level, knowing and understanding the broader picture with regard to expectations for behaviour provided an overall foundation for devising individualised forms of care. Achieving a balance in the pace at which this was brought about was important, as shown in the next example:

> [We] have a care planning sheet for the linkworker with the young person and we break it down into the dimensions of the LAC [Looking After Children] documents so you have health, education and so forth, and it's just to give us an opportunity maybe once a month to sit and talk about that in person, me and them on a one-to-one 'Where are you with this?' you know 'What do they want about that?' you know. It's the checks about 'Are health things being seen to? Education, planning for the future, leisure, whatever other work' and the member of staff then also shares that with the young person so they have the [communication] flow all ways so everyone's involved in it but I find that gives me a chance to say, right, to maybe direct what could or should be being done [laughing] where they should be up to and what should be happening and to avoid the drift as well which you can, as I say, things haven't got to be done at a frantic pace but there's a danger I think when you're looking after people for a few years that you think, ooh I've got plenty of time and you actually don't achieve anything.

Part of the manager's role involved ensuring that all aspects of care planning were being carried out by the designated person.

Establishing boundaries and routines for young people

Formal expectations

Working to procedural guidelines was important. Many managers made this awareness a first priority: things must be done 'by the book'. This was particularly the case for those working in small groups of homes where hierarchical tiers were closely interrelated, as in some independent sector homes. Ensuring that staff were secure in their understanding of both statutory and organisational expectations for young people's behaviour was seen as a foundation from which confident practice was most likely to ensue. Such a foundation was sometimes seen as being guaranteed by the provision of training manuals or induction packs, which often contained checklists of some sort:

> There is a keyworker file that we have that describes the role of the keyworker... We also have obviously a quite, quite involved file of policies and procedures that all our staff are conscious of; it's part of their training and induction to be aware of all those policies and procedures. So to be honest I would say that the vast majority of our staff group know

what they can say, what they can do, whether they're speaking with a social worker or a parent or whatever and each of them has a degree of autonomy to be honest. I think each member of staff knows they have my full backing on any decision they might make, you know, providing they've gone through the various procedures that one would expect... And we have a very involved, what we call induction pack which is effectively a three-month training manual that all new members of staff have to go through and there are lots and lots of questions 'What would you do if...?' for instance, and the only way they can find out is to go to the policies and procedures file and find out the answer, and that is checked off [as completed] at the end of three months by a team leader and by myself and [a third senior member of staff].

In some organisations, emphasis was placed on young people themselves being given written guidance as to expectations for ways of behaving, forming a counterpart to the guidance given to staff:

Young people receive a welcome booklet which kind of details sort of the rules of the house and what they're expected to do, their pocket money, their bedtime and of course this is all discussed when they come to visit as well. So that sort of nothing's a real shock to them when they come in and it's all about boundary setting and keeping tight boundaries to ensure that they stick to the rules of the house and they've got those, they've got their own copy of the welcome booklet, they've got them there and they have a [young persons'] meeting once a week so that they can sit and chat and ask us questions, things that they'd like to be implemented and we take that to our team meeting. So it's about working with them.

This kind of formal introduction to the home and its way of working was more prominently profiled in small groups of homes in the independent sector, where it was used as a welcoming orientation for young people who were usually placed at some distance away from their relatives, friends and social networks. The idea of young people being overtly aware of an agreement to ways of behaving was more formalised within particular independent sector small group provisions, and within those small local authority homes which laid emphasis on (as distinct from specialised in) particular aspects of care, such as preparation for independence.

Negotiating boundaries

'Establishing boundaries' for, or 'testing boundaries' by young people, were terms used in varying degrees of definition by managers. Some boundaries were regarded as negotiable, others, usually related to risk, were termed 'non-negotiable'. At times 'establishing boundaries' meant identifying tight, clear rules, while in other cases use of the term related to identifying extreme points, reached only after young people passed beyond demonstrating a wide variety of behaviours of increasing cause for concern. Whatever way the term was used, it was always in conjunction with identifying ways of managing or controlling behaviour, as shown in the next two examples:

> They [young people] accept the boundaries for what they are and they understand when we impose a sanction that there's a good reason for it and we always sit down, if we have had an incident or a physical intervention with the young person there'll always be an independent person goes through the report with them, someone that wasn't there dealing with the situation. So they get to give their side of it and put their views across and most of the time the young people will always come and apologise to people afterwards, which is a big thing for them I think. Nobody finds it easy to apologise and it's quite a big thing and it shows how much they do respect people that they've got the nerve to come and do it. They're very good like that.

> We find a lot of the children that come here, they need a lot of stability in their life, they need a lot of routine and they need a lot of boundaries, and we gain restraint training if we do have to hold a young person, and the only time you would hold is if they became very seriously threatening or hurting yourself or if they were threatening themselves or hurting themselves or if there was severe damage to the property. What we would try to do is talking, compromising, they have goals plans so we try to set goals for them, small rewards, it may be one big reward like one boy's been able to go to school for two weeks, which is a mainstream school which we've got him back into… And he did his half a day and he came back and we made a really big fuss of him and he went out and bought himself a single CD from us and that was a little reward for him.

Boundaries were viewed as forming part of a structure, giving security to young people and a sense of direction to staff. Approaches to establishing and maintaining boundaries varied according to degrees of influence on practice of the organisation or department in which the home operated, and degrees of influence exerted by managers. For some homes, levels of complex and demanding work were consistently high. All managers regarded this as part and parcel of the residential task, and a key challenge was to convince staff of this and enable them to adopt clear ways of working with such demands:

> We have a 12-year-old, for instance, he's got a lot of needs, he needs to feel safe so we've spent a lot of time talking about how rules and boundaries can actually contribute towards his feeling of security and safety, and just because you're constantly being challenged as an adult doesn't mean that there's something fundamentally wrong with him or with what we're doing, that's the way it is and that's what we're here for. So we shouldn't get stressed out that we're getting a lot of it.

Often staff drew first on their own experience of young people's behaviour, set in the context of their own histories, and defined acceptable behaviour from that point. Considerable amounts of managers' time was spent turning this around by helping staff to empathise with resident young people as a prior condition for establishing expectations for behaviour in the home, and thereby appropriate boundaries:

> So if a child doesn't want to go to bed then you can pick up pretty quickly whether they're just playing games with you or whether there's a reason there and if there's a reason there then, you know, you can sit and you can work through that. It might be that, certainly within the first few nights of them coming in, you can predict that they're not going to want to go to bed because it's frightening and those, those are the discussions that we have in a staff meeting with regard to the children about how they would feel, we try and get the staff to empathise as much as possible with 'When you first came into work, how did you feel? Well, you know, multiply that by a few thousand and you'll get how a child feels being taken from everything that's familiar'. So we try and create that kind of culture.

Identifying the state of each young person as they came to live in the home provided the starting point for relationship-forming and for establishing familiarity, routine and boundaries for behaviour.

Using systems of reward

Reward systems were variously utilised according to the situation. Sometimes it was the case that managers had initiated this, while others had inherited a token economy which they did not favour, but which they felt unable to abolish because it was part of the approach used by sister homes, or it was liked by the young people. In other cases managers brought such ways of operating to the home after having used them successfully in previous situations.

In those homes where education was integral to the organisation, relationships between the children's home and its education counterpart varied.

Many children's homes managers sought to form close relationships with teaching staff, and this was achieved with varying degrees of success. In one situation in our sample, the two forms of provision were inseparable in terms of management structure and operation, and were located on the same site; ways of managing behaviour were linked to this, as shown in the following quotation:

> We believe education is at the core of what we do here. A lot of the reward structures that we have for young people we've systematically based them in the school. So if the young people wish to earn extra bits and pieces then it depends on their school work and their attitude to education. So everything is geared towards education. We've also gone along the line of instituting things like open days and so on and we have regular meetings between care staff and teachers; updating care plans always includes education, care and therapy for instance, and we have these [meetings] on a regular basis.

Throughout the sample, staff and managers alike were keen to monitor their use of sanction and reward, as early recourse to the former was seen as counterproductive, although it was a fairly frequent response in the face of changes, or from inexperienced staff lacking in confidence:

> We've perhaps dished out more sanctions over the last, well, five months than normal but we've had a new young person come in and it's about learning to live together again and getting used to the new resident and the new resident getting used to the others and how we work and what the boundaries are.

Some remained unconvinced of the merit of sanction or reward as a behavioural change agent, yet were committed to its benefit in terms of providing a clear approach to helping young people discriminate between different forms of behaviour and their acceptability:

> We have an incentive scheme for our younger residents, the ones of school age, where their school attendance and behaviour is sort of linked to a points scheme where they can earn points for goodies and outings and things like that [pause] and I've got very mixed feelings about that, you know. I mean I'm not a great fan of a sort of token economy which is what it is. But the kids like it. [Pause] I mean one of the things I think it actually succeeded in doing and it's good for young people whose experience of life and relationships have been chaotic, it introduces a certain amount of predictability and certainty into life. So you've actually got a written bit of paper that says 'If you do what you're supposed to do and you go to

school, you earn 50 points, you know, and that with those 50 points you can do x, y and z, and if you go to bed on time you get however many points' and it works like that. And [pause] quite a large percentage of kids will buy into this and really like it, they'll come in several times a day to check how many points they've got [pause] I think what it also does for them is it makes a very clear statement about what sort of behaviour we want to encourage, what sort of behaviour is good and what sort of behaviour nobody likes. That doesn't mean to say that they always behave themselves because I think sometimes different agendas will cause them to choose to behave in ways that we would be, regard as undesirable, but I think that's a different thing. I think we've still got the basic idea that these behaviours here, these are what we want you to do and we'll reward you, and the others you don't [get rewarded for].

Many staff and managers were relaxed about the kinds of reward systems in use, framing these in terms of goal-setting:

[…]quite often if there's something they particularly want we'll do a goal for a couple of weeks and then go out and buy something if it's a reasonable price, or it might just be going out for a cup of coffee or a cup of hot chocolate, going out somewhere special that they particularly want to go to.

Others felt themselves to have little freedom of choice in the way they worked with specific young people's behaviour, where history and advice from external sources promoted early responses with which they were not always comfortable:

And in some cases we do feel at times your hands are tied – i.e. Monday morning one of our new little lads was in bed, totally refusing to get out for school, being extremely verbally abusive, this young man's only just come out of secure and in his 28-day review his social worker was saying, you know, 'We need to maintain firm boundaries round him because if not he tends to go absolutely wild'. So what we decided to do quickly with him was to withdraw the things that he particularly liked to do, and that evening he wasn't allowed to go into the computer room and I think he also received an early bed and that was his sanction and the next day thankfully he went to school. But at the same time, although we did pull back the computer and an early bed, what we all felt worked well, if there's a trip going out let's take him out, and that's what we did and it did work on that occasion.

Sanction and reward were often contextualised alongside the aim of providing a learning experience for young people in terms of responsibility:

Running alongside that and it's something that I feel really strongly about is helping young people to develop a sense of responsibility. We've had a lot of procedures and stuff issued about children's rights, and their rights in care and this sort of thing and I mean I just believe so much that where you have rights you have responsibilities and I think, a fundamental part of teaching young people to develop into the sort of adults I would hope they will is teaching them about their responsibilities to other people.

The operation of systems of reward were by no means straightforward to maintain, and frequently managers were called upon to monitor the practice of staff, or to mediate, or overturn staff decisions. Explaining to staff the manager's own rationale behind particular responses to behaviour was frequently required:

Most of these youngsters come from difficult backgrounds, otherwise they wouldn't be in the care system and, you know, you're expected to kind of make a change within their lives, but the philosophy that you may have for an older group is not going to be the same as for a younger group. So the message goes out the window slightly, you get somebody with extreme behaviour problems I guess put in with kids who are quite settled, you're going to get the different messages with that person because you're slightly managing that person differently. For example, if they're kind of abusive all the time…people might say 'Well, what do you do about it?' Yes, we don't condone it, you know, we give them the right messages, we try and counsel them and all those issues, do you impose sanctions, yes we do, depending. But somebody who's displaying these extreme behaviours, are you going to sanction them every second, then [you get] somebody [else] who swears now and then you're saying 'Come on, that's totally inappropriate'. But youngsters may get different messages that you're not doing the same things to the other one as you're doing to someone with this extreme behaviour.

Achieving staff consistency in responses to the behaviour of young people was an ongoing task.

Working with changing needs

Keeping in touch with the pace of development of both young people and staff was crucial, in order to plan, co-ordinate and communicate what was needed at any given time for each young person. This was not achieved simply:

And with certain young people there needs to be a high level of control where, the other young people, we've worked through those control issues and those no longer seem to be particularly significant. Every now and again they raise their head but, how much we've had to put controls in and very rigid boundaries around young people that shifts as they, as they learn, as they mature, as they change, as they grow, as things around them change, I think. There's lots of reasons why.

Recognition of the need for flexibility and areas suitable for negotiation on the part of staff in relation to young people had to be given careful consideration if these were to work with a degree of consistency throughout the home:

You have different, different attitudes and different approaches and I think that's quite right too, you know, I don't think any of us would want a team of people who were, were all the same…there's always…a desire, quite rightly, to get consistency, you know, consistency in the way things are dealt with and with some staff this will push for rules that are written on tablets of stone, you know. 'That's a rule and so you can't do so-and-so because the rule says so', you know, and that to me precludes any negotiation around particular circumstances or reasons why things might be different. I mean we do have, we, I think we've, we've done a lot of work on which things are absolute no-no's and which things might be negotiable, you know.

Working with different needs at different times with different staff posed complex challenges to managers' skills in terms of communicating their preferred approach.

Being seen to be fair was an important issue, and one which merited explanation to young people and staff alike, as can be seen clearly in the following example:

I think my biggest difficulty, and some of this is not just from me but it's been from inspection reports and changing philosophies as well, it's [about] the rewarding good behaviour rather than the sanctions for the bad behaviour or the unwanted behaviour, and I think that is something that I find at times I, I'm arguing my corner a fair bit on that because people say 'Well, they've done this and there has to be a consequence'. Well yes there does but if they did something on Sunday the consequence doesn't have to be they don't get their pocket money the following Friday and that is the one at times that I can see, and those people at times, that they are just feeling sometimes that that is just being soft. And then you find very surprisingly somebody comes from the point of view that you've been trying to put forward and argue [laughing…'a convert'].

Our point here is that establishing boundaries and routines was set within a fluid context, where expectations had to take account of individual needs from within a group setting. Prioritisation of consistency over individual needs or vice versa was a matter for judgement. Part of the manager's task was to make tangible the preferred rationale for decision making in relation to approaches used. This explanatory process related to both staff and young people, in varying degrees and ways, according to the situation.

Building relationships with young people

The security of staff knowing accepted ways to proceed and behave formed part of building an understanding relationship with each young person. Apparently simple in intent, relationship-building was one of the most crucial and complex areas of practice, taking time, insight and patience to achieve successfully. Arguably, forming an understanding relationship was viewed as the primary residential task. Sometimes this was seen to occur as almost incidental to a young person arriving at the home and taking their place within the group after receiving a welcome booklet or the like, but most often this was part of a thought-out but unforced approach, as in the following instance, given at length in order to illustrate some of the dimensions of the task over time:

> Care and consideration for children are really important and we start it from the word go in the way that we introduce children I think. So there's introductory packs, there's the settling at bedtime with stories, there's the making sure that they've got everything that they need in a material sense, that their bedrooms are nice, they've had some choice in, and even bits of things before we even think about, you know, what they're really like. Taking them out and buying a magazine and a poster to put up in their bedroom, it's that, ensuring that, you know, we give a message even though children don't always verbalise and we can't say it to them, that message is very clear to me about 'We want you here'. So I think the other thing is that, you know, right through my career, I've been very reluctant to use the word 'restraint' because I think it becomes a culture and I also think that on the whole you can reason with children. It may take some time and you might have to sit out, sit with it for a long time but I think you can actually reason with them. So when you're looking at aggressive behaviour it's trying to put some responsibility back on the child. Some of the techniques that we use for that is remove other children and let the child come to terms and go through that aggressive cycle, and the coming down, making sure that you're still there. Not actually backing children

into a corner either so that they have to come out fighting. So it's the words that you use I think as well as the action that you take in that 'I know that you're feeling very angry, I'm not sure whether you're angry with me but I'm going to give you a bit of time just to calm down and I'll come back'. Where children have fallen out with each other it's like 'I think we need to break this up, I think we need to get away from each other'. It sounds very easy and it's not, it's very, very complex, very complicated. The other bit of that, what we do is we concentrate on positive behaviour and rewarding positive behaviour. So putting something in place there for a child to work to rather than taking something away.

Working from within an overtly recognised regulatory framework, managers retained sight of a balance between longer-term goals for young people and the appropriate pace for each child:

We work to policies and procedures and statutory sort of law really. So we'd only work within that forum. It's about building up the relationship with the child, so that if the child kicks off, as they say, that you're able to work with that child after the child's been through the physical, through the violence, you're able to actually bring that child down and work with that child. And within that you should see a child coming in from day one to a child leaving you when all that has decreased because of the work that's been put in, because, staff can identify when a child's going to lose it or lose control and they can work with that child prior to it getting to the level that it would have prior to coming into [our home].

A sense of progress on behalf of the young person was viewed as a major part of the residential task.

The role of keyworkers

Keyworkers or linkworkers were seen as vital to developing relationships successfully with young people. Most usually, a keyworker acted as the person with lead responsibility for the young person and, where present, a linkworker acted as a bridge in the absence of the keyworker. Keyworkers would usually adopt the role of main communicators in relation to others involved with the young person, such as other professional bodies, other statutory and voluntary agencies, and would be likely to attend planning meetings perhaps in addition to senior staff from the home who held more decision-making responsibilities:

The keyworker is the person who would take ultimate responsibility for that particular child, to record all their daily requirements of maybe doctor's appointments, this sort of thing, to keep a record of those to ensure that the young person goes, they will prepare reports for reviews, they will contact parents and social workers. And they would advise other staff and myself and Mark [another senior] of what was happening with the young person. So there's a lot of delegation of authority of that sort of work, communication with social workers down to the keyworker. The keyworker is only on one shift so there's two days when they're available and four days when they're not. So we believe a linkworker is necessary should anything untoward occur and the young person might then wish to contact, or have a word with the linkworker but often you'll find, they will pass it on to a keyworker and they might either phone the young person or come in or give something, whatever's necessary, to be honest, to work with them.

Young people thus had an identified individual worker who would prioritise their interests within the home and who could be relied on to act as their representative across the boundary of the home. Young people sometimes were able to exercise choice in selecting their keyworkers:

For every young person we have, they are allocated a keyworker. Initially when they join us we allocate a keyworker from one of our seniors but that's only for a period of a couple of weeks while the young person gets to know members of staff; then they can choose the keyworker that they wish to work for them and the linkworker on another shift.

The extent to which the keyworker system was prioritised varied according to other prevailing concerns. Making space to work with specific young people was not always possible in the face of high level of demand from others in the resident group. Calm patches were seen to provide opportunities for developing the relationship with the young person and providing one-to-one support:

I mean it's so settled at the moment that what we're finding is if you're working and your key child's around you're getting the opportunity to be able to spend an hour with them just on your own and the other member of staff can sort of, you know, sit around with the other, with the other four or five kids, which we've not had in an unsettled period, which is quite nice at the moment, you're finding more time with your key child.

High levels of demand from young people meant that attention at times was focused on particular young people, or the group as a whole, and not necessarily on the child who was perceived as needing attention or, more simply, on the plan for the day.

Most usually, keyworking involved work internal and external to the home. Working across the boundary of the home, and enabling others so to do, formed a large part of the manager's role in respect of achieving the best for the young people living in the home. Knowing about and understanding ways of working with other professionals such as those from employment or housing departments usually involved the manager's input to a high degree. It was most often the case that instigating and maintaining action from other professionals was heavily dependent on the efforts of residential staff. Enabling staff to operate confidently within external professional networks required detailed work in advance. Some managers preferred to be directly involved in the majority of external relationships:

> As manager you're expected to be, and so you should be, at all the reviews, at the key meetings, whether it's health, mental health reviews and, and partnership meetings or education liaison functions, that whole range, neighbours' meetings, community liaison meetings, we have one of those on a regular basis where we meet with all the neighbours to address issues, police liaison. It's pretty endless really and that's not even taking into account training.

Others quite clearly managed the practice of their staff who were engaged in work outside the home by undertaking detailed preparatory work in advance of action:

> If a member of staff's going to a meeting with a social worker or a school they'd only be going into a meeting if I felt confident in the way they could present themselves in an appropriate professional manner and they knew what they were talking about. I always brief staff beforehand, you know, about issues that may arise and I always make it clear that if they can't answer something then they have to say that they need to refer back to me. But because they're briefed beforehand they've got most things in place.

These two approaches were seen to be in operation in combination at times, sometimes a matter of convenience, sometimes through preference. Few managers were in the position to rely routinely on representation outside the home taking place without their involvement in some form, although there were exceptions in respect of certain senior staff:

> Well I certainly would expect them [senior staff] to be meeting with the families and actually attending reviews and be meeting with field social workers to discuss cases without my being involved in every instance, and I guess that the more complex cases I would dip in and out of really. In

terms of, if it's a complex care meeting and it needs that more complex decision making or contribution from myself then I would be there.

Almost all managers were involved at the starting point with any external relationship, and viewed topping-up that relationship as part of their own task, as advocate for and representative of the home.

External relationships in respect of working with young people took many forms. Our focus here is on those of most concern to managers – namely, with field social workers and those involved in education. Relationships 'across the boundary of the home' formed a considerable part of the manager's role, and although from time to time these were perceived as drawing managers away from the central task within the home, it was the case that these were seen in a more positive light than reported in previous research (Whitaker *et al.* 1998):

> I think by putting a big focus on the partnership approach to the work that, that we're not there just to do everything and, you know, replicate a parenting situation where, you know, you're the parent and you do everything, we actually work in partnership with the families, the field social workers and education to a higher degree than, than a parent would as a norm perhaps and that by developing those partnership approaches you ensure I think that, that your task and the way you approach it is, is attended to properly and in the correct spirit of approaches to residential child care because you have your partnership agencies around you who are offering a degree of scrutiny and monitoring of, of what you, what you're doing and how you're approaching it. So I think if you do have good practice on that you're ensuring that, you know, that you're heading in the right direction, cos if you're not people are going to tell you, you know.

Outreach work and work in partnership with other organisations was by and large welcomed as part of the residential task and seen to play a part in maintaining appropriately permeable boundaries around the home:

> I've always been one that believes strongly in working with everybody. Whatever's going to give the kids the best service then I'm going to work with them. I feel one of the best things I can do and I haven't got that ingrained yet here but I'm hoping in time, once the staff are trained up properly and, and can do things like family work and group work, but I want them trained, I don't want, you know, them just, you know, flying off and doing something, that they do it in tandem with field workers, that we work together and it's joint efforts. When I was doing some of the abuse work I did it with field social workers, I've done family work with

field social workers, they'd come in at six o'clock at night and we would sit and we'd do family work. So I think the, the positives are working with other agencies, whether it be clinical, whether it be field, whether it be the medical staff or, or whatever.

The main point to take from this is that throughout our research managers welcomed the greater opportunities which now existed in relation to inter-agency working. They welcomed the greater control over co-ordinating services that they felt their role now represented. Further to this, many held optimistic views about the benefits which the registration of residential managers would bring to their potential for operating, citing control over purpose and function as the main area of importance.

Developing and maintaining relationships with others

There were many examples given to us of ways in which managers and staff worked across the boundaries of children's homes – for example, with families, professionals and other organisations. Here we choose to focus on two of the most commonly held arenas of practice in which developing and maintaining relationships with others was highly important – namely, with field social workers and with schools.

Relationships with field social workers

Perceptions of the importance of regular contact with field social workers varied considerably, according to the degrees of freedom felt or taken by the manager of the home and/or the wider organisation. Field social workers were most involved at the point of placement for young people and, although they occupied a very important role during the course of the placement, many managers felt that they and their staff were equipped to undertake many of the tasks which more traditionally formed part of the field social workers' role, such as family reunification work. In those cases managers were happy for their staff to carry out such tasks, as they regarded them as being more appropriate to those with residential insight. Further to this, in some organisations, residential managers and staff seemed to involve field social workers as a matter of courtesy, keeping them informed of progress and concerns about young people, and checking that things were on course:

I'm afraid they [field social workers] step back a bit [when a young person is placed here]. Whereas perhaps in other places they benefit more from (pause) regular social work appearances, we don't. We have to really, I suppose really, you know, when you think about it we do a lot more because we do their role too. A young man just moved on from here and went with one of us to where he was going, we did the, we did the shopping, we did everything and he moved on with a member of staff from here cos there was no social worker available. The aftercare worker was on the sick so we did it, and our young lady who's moving into foster care, we found the foster parents. So we did it.

Where greater accountability to field social workers was felt, more routine contact was thought to be essential. This level of accountability was seen to be highest in the independent sector, where the field social worker often acted as both conduit to the family context and representative of the commissioning organisation, both of which were often at some distance from the young person's children's home:

We have a system really where we contact our social workers on a weekly basis and whoever's on, it's a Monday morning, whoever's on on a Monday morning has the responsibility to phone them and we just give them a general update every week. Discuss anything that might have arose during the period in time. We liaise with them about the home visits and any activities that they want to do, cos obviously we have to get their consent for every activity that's outside the norm. I mean they sign forms for activity consents but we have to check everything out to make sure that they approve, you know… Sometimes, sometimes you tend to, you know, keep ringing and ringing and leaving messages. Other times you'll ring and you'll get them straight away. I have to say the ones that we're dealing with at the moment are very good, if we've rung and left a message they will get back to us. We have had some in the past that, you know, you can ring all week and you'll have no joy till the next week and, you know, it's unfortunate but you, you do appreciate at the same time just how busy they are but at the same time we don't want our young people to be neglected and if it's just for the sake of a phone call, you know, we want to know that they're there, they're up to date, they're up to speed, so, so as to allay any problems.

Given that field social workers were frequently used as reference points in this way in our sample, the corresponding concern widely identified about lack of *allocated* social workers is an area worthy of further research exploration and understanding. The impact of this lack was considerable:

Probably one of the most difficult areas sometimes and I think it's become more evident in the last five to six months and I think more so because of the current climate in terms of there aren't enough social workers around, you see the amount of people that, the amount of children that we care for that sometimes don't have allocated social workers. Or they have to keep cancelling reviews… If it goes too long I'll then write a letter and I'll express all my concerns and I'll share some of my sympathy with their demands of their job but unfortunately I have a target to meet which is making sure this young person has a statutory review within a certain time. It's imperative he knows where he's going, it's imperative that people have a clear understanding of their role and responsibility within his care plan and I also think it's very important that the parents and the guardians and the social worker and the Chair, and all the other people that work with this person know why, where the young person is in terms of whether they're doing well, whether they're just managing it or whether they're not. And I think it's important that people know, and very often if you're not careful it will drift and we work very, and again that's that progress chasing, and we work very, and that's frustrating because I can't always get an answer, you know. Sometimes we're ringing up and talking to people that are on duty because the case is being handled by duty. Now a duty worker today may not be the same duty worker as tomorrow.

In our sample of children's homes, it was the case that 27 young people were without an allocated field social worker at the second point of data collection (see Chapter 2), a factor which had widespread implications for the young people, their families, residential staff and their organisations.

Relationships with schools

The importance of the role of education in relation to the future life chances for looked after young people is undisputed and in particular attention has been drawn to those living in residential care (Jackson and Martin 1998). Many young people leave the care system without qualifications (Dixon and Stein 2005; Stein 1990). In our research, developing and maintaining relationships with schools was regarded as a vital part of the manager's task. Enabling young people to attend mainstream school was seen as a positive goal not easily achieved once disruption had occurred for the young person. Those homes with access to their own schools also sought mainstream provision where possible. Although some homes were able to be selective in their admissions criteria in respect of young people's school attendance, the majority of homes experienced difficulties in sustaining attendance for certain young people. The reasons for this varied, from the level of the individual young person's motivation, to difficulties presented at a particular school, to difficulties held at more bureaucratic levels, such as funding for transport.

Whatever the reason for difficulty, integrating the young person within the school was seen clearly to lie with the home itself as distinct from being the responsibility of professionals within the education system. The extent to which managers were able to contend with difficulty in this respect varied.

At an individual level, the case of the 14-year-old described in the following quotation illustrates that successful negotiations had taken place over time in order to achieve eventually a mainstream placement. As far as the manager could ascertain, the young person had not attended school since she was six years old:

> One of the reasons for her move over to [here] was because we already had a link with a mainstream school and we have a good relationship with them and it's quite often easier to get the young people in if you've already established a good working relationship because these, the school systems aren't easy, you know. I mean even having that link it was still a long, you know, I mean it, she moved in here in February but it's took till July to actually get her through the system. So that's quite a lengthy period of time for a young person when they're sitting waiting to go and they're chomping at the bit to get out of here and because of the delays, you know, it did affect her and she did get wound up by it and, you know, she thought it wasn't going to happen and she began to doubt her own ability. But again we just kept working at it, kept ploughing away and, you know, we would just sit and talk, and the same with her tutor about what she would be doing and what she wouldn't be doing at school and what things she had to do in regards to keeping her cool, you know, if the teachers said something she didn't like to hear, you know. We spent a lot of time around those sorts of subjects. And really…so far so good really. She's gone off and it's not been a problem, she's settled in well and the school are quite pleased… To get her into mainstream was an incredibly big step for her and for us, you know. To have two [out of three] young people that are away from the house in proper school, you know, it's brilliant.

Sometimes a proactive stance was held formally, and in partnership with others, and this was regarded as a positive step en route to resolving individual difficulties with education:

> It's a big problem getting the young people into education especially if they can't maintain mainstream education in terms of their abilities. Mainstream schools are reluctant to say the least to take young people in care.

So that, that is always a huge obstacle. There's a…corporate parenting group that liaise with us and with schools, they're part of the education department and they, we work very, very closely with them now…we do quite a lot of sort of networking and liaising with local schools, we also, there's a locality panel meeting once every six weeks or so and there are people from education, people from planning and admissions who, who sit round and discuss any particular children that we're having particular problems with and they will all put their heads together and try and come up with ways, or sorts of things, that we can put in place to help.

At a more general level, the following manager illustrates an active, informal approach towards resolving difficulties, with residential staff acting in line with what would ordinarily be regarded as a parenting role:

I mean obviously there's hiccups and there's glitches and there's links that we have to make with schools when things are not going so well but that's just issues around good corporate parenting, you know, that's around my staff doing what they would do for their own children and if things go wrong at school then you don't wait for a social worker going in there you actually go down, kick the door down metaphorically of the school and you work with, you know, as if it was your own, as if it was your own child and the staff have got a very good handle on that, to be fair, and they deal with the issues and the, and the difficulties at source and they deal with them very swiftly and I think that works very well when you're, you know, when you're talking about providing support to young people and the young people know what the expectations are when they come into [this home] and the support around education.

A complicating factor across the board was having to balance the needs of the group with those of the individual:

This young man who they're [the school] refusing to have in at the moment, we could have made a big fuss and sort of taken him up and insisted that he'd gone there but that wouldn't have helped him. It wouldn't have helped our relationships with the school, because I have another young lady who attends there and had a 100 per cent attendance last term, you know, so I thought, we don't want to put up barriers, you know, but we still want this young man, you know, to get a fair deal, to have some education.

Managers overall had fairly low expectations of schools in relation to their initial willingness to work with difficulties being experienced by young people from their homes. This presented crucial challenges in terms of negotiating acceptability, and providing support. Many managers were in the position of having to establish relationships and work towards organising things as they would like them to be. Frustrations in this respect abounded, as one manager with long-standing experience indicated:

> We are in constant meetings and deliberations with schools because a lot of my children are either half-day pupils or have been excluded from the mainstream of the school. So we're in constant battles with education over proper education for the young people, tutors have been promised and not forthcoming, increase in non-attending and we're going to lots of meetings, and I use my learning support teacher, he comes along with us because sometimes they listen to an educationalist quicker than they do a residential worker for some reason, and I've attended personally several of the meetings at one school and actually saved the bacon for a young lady who's now in fostering and doing very well who had a very troubled and turbulent life and is attending school regularly and doing very well. But other schools are, some are better than others. We have input into a system where they have a panel...which is actually [about] pupil inclusion and, and looking at any issues that are cropping up. I haven't seen it do much in helping us but at least it's there and we're attending and, and we go to school meetings and, and parents' nights and try and keep in with the schools as much as possible. We've allowed children to come back rather than be excluded on occasions for a time out period but some have tried to abuse it so I've started saying 'No, you either exclude, or that child –', I mean one because she didn't wear her shoes or something, and I said 'No, you're not sending her home for that, thank you very much'.

For those young people for whom school did not seem to be possible or appropriate at that time, it was seen as important to give focus to the time which was being spent out of school. This took many forms:

> And I suppose from a sort of practical angle what I like the staff to do is to, even when the young people are out of school is to try and provide education structure, in inverted commas if you like, where...we try and maintain a daily routine that involves some form of education but it's not about sitting down and doing maths, it's about looking at different ways of doing it. It's about, you know, timetabling, you go shopping with the staff then and that's, that's a sort of maths, it's a sort of life skills and it's also, you know, allowing them either one-to-one time with staff to talk through issues. There's a number of different things you will get out of, I suppose when I first came the young people who didn't attend school were being sat down with worksheets in maths and they were getting very little out of it. Asking the staff to understand that, you know, going

swimming with a young person isn't necessarily a treat, it's, there's a number of different things you can get out of it.

Over time, it was the case that managers of some homes had achieved what they regarded as positive and successful ways of working in respect of approaches to education:

> Every one of my children goes to school, every one of them completes homework when they return home. We all, all staff attend parents' evening, we go to watch them in sport races, we go into school if there's problems, we have regular meetings and I think that's important that the children see that but education's important to them and, you know, that's why I push it very, very strongly…we make school a very positive experience for the children. When we do homework we do child-focused work with them so we may, we do theme nights, so we'll do a lot of cultural work with getting them to paint flags and talk about food from that particular country and they enjoy that sort of stuff. We make it, you know, fun to learn.

Sometimes unwillingness to accept a young person into school was overt on the part of the school:

> We've just been saying today, with a headmistress at the school up the road who's asked for one of our young people to have to leave from now until she finishes school in June [two months' time]. And we're sort of, we're fighting a battle with that one, about 'Well is she excluded?' 'No she's not', well if she's not excluded she should be able to go to school.

At other times, blocks to acceptance were more difficult to ascertain, and therefore to resolve:

> There sometimes may be a school but the school don't actually want them but they're not being as honest as to say they're excluding them.

Although greater willingness by schools to co-operate with residential staff than in previous years was reported in this research, almost all managers had to concentrate and work hard on relationships with schools at some point. This often took the form of assisting teachers to manage behaviour, and defuse potentially problematic situations:

> I will go to the school and speak to the youngster and cool the situation down and try and keep them at the school and work with the teachers and sometimes the youngster knowing that the adults are there kind of diffuses the situation rather than just leaving it and, and the situation escalating and the school rings and says 'This child's been excluded for three

days, you know, as a cooling off period, will you pick them up?' But some schools work quite closely in the sense they'll ring us up and say 'Can you come and have a chat with this youngster?' you know. In one particular one where I went a week ago and he was kicking off and the teacher says 'Can you take him away because he's been a nuisance all morning' and I had about ten minutes with him, just to praise him to say how well he was, I said 'Look you've done quite well last year, you've had a 100 per cent attendance, excellent, do you really want to mess it up in your final year?' and he calmed right down. That was a kind of good example, you know, and he was all right for the afternoon. So in that sense the schools are working more closely with us and trying to, and I think the teachers are becoming more aware as well that, you know, these youngsters actually come from difficult backgrounds and the first response shouldn't be, you know, 'Take them away'.

This kind of external work usually fell into the ambit of the manager or senior staff for negotiation, and often managers themselves played a direct part in relation to the young person and to staff at the relevant school. Helping teachers and residential staff together to identify opportunities for working constructively with young people in this respect was clearly a key task for managers.

Summary

This is the last of our three chapters focusing on the process of managing children's homes. Here we have built on insights from previous research (Berridge 2002; Berridge and Brodie 1998; Brown *et al.* 1998; Clough 2000; Sinclair and Gibbs 1998a; Whitaker *et al.* 1998) in developing an understanding of the ways managers bring about work in relation to the young people in their care.

Holding clear objectives from the outset, enabled by clear procedural guidelines and expectations, promoted harmonious working relationships between staff and a likely sense of security for young people. Moreover, for-mulating a distinctive approach to working with young people to which all were able to adhere made for greater certainty and therefore confidence in practice.

In respect of the needs of young people, it was clear that managers deter-mined approaches to these by taking account of the capabilities of their staff. Knowing and understanding young people's needs and characteristics requires participation from and direction by managers in relation to the staff group. Managers collaborate with their staff in respect of establishing boundaries and routines for young people which take account of individuals as well as the group, using sanction and reward processes where deemed appropriate. Success is dependent upon a mixture of formal means, such as keyworker and review systems, and informal means, such as building relationships.

Building relationships with young people with and through keyworkers and linkworkers is a necessary precondition for active work within the home and with networks external to the home. Additionally, with others such as field social workers and schools, building relationships and negotiating and maintaining boundaries are both dynamic and vital.

The skills required of managers in relation to working with young people are diverse. In sum, this chapter shows that managers must provide strong reference points for young people and direction for strategic working with them. They also act as role models for work with young people, act as advocates for them and for the home itself, and as general external representatives for the home. They interact across the boundary of their homes and encourage others to do so. They must be experienced over time with their homes, and be capable of shaping their teams and team members without treating them as objects. As we have seen in previous chapters, managers must be able to command loyalty and bring about motivation and commitment, protect all from the negative effects of external forces, and, perhaps above all, be experts in relationships and in containing anxiety.

How do differences come into play in the management of children's homes? Before moving on to looking at what influences the ways that resources are used, in the next chapter we examine the crucial distinctions in the ways homes are managed. We show the ways that data from the qualitative part of our research have been used, and the implications this analysis has for our focus on the concept of leadership itself.

Chapter 6

What Does Leadership Look Like in Children's Homes?

Introduction

The previous three chapters have provided detailed accounts of what the role of the manager of a children's home entails. On the basis of these accounts, the current chapter turns to our analysis of the role in terms of the elements contained in an overall conceptualisation of leadership in children's homes. We begin by considering the implications of theories of leadership and leadership development. We build on these in our thinking about the main approaches used by managers and their links to the interdependent levels of influence brought to bear on their tasks. We end the chapter by looking at what our data told us about where differences lie in the execution of the task of managing children's homes. We show that it is possible to distinguish between areas of strength and weakness and thereby form a qualitative assessment of what constitutes successful practice.

What implications are there for children's homes in terms of theories of leadership and leadership development?

Our initial hypotheses involved the notion that, in order to manage children's homes successfully, managers had to function as more than good administrators and supervisors of daily tasks operating from within fixed budgets. We have described the extent to which managers had to keep their fingers on the pulses of their children's homes, build and develop their teams, and model practice with young people. We have seen also the extent to which managers acted or were able to act as leaders of their teams.

We have noted previously our use of the term 'manager' or 'residential manager' as distinct from 'head of home'. The terms have slightly differing implications. Headship (as in 'head of home'), and for that matter 'manager', denotes authority by referring to the most senior role in an executive hierarchy. Leadership, put simply, may be seen as denoting influence. In children's homes, authoritative work takes place that is not merely a matter for the manager, or a case of distinction between the roles of leader and follower. Work takes place that is fast-paced and interrupted, and cannot wait for the 'right' person to be present. Practitioners need to know the way things are expected to be done and by whom, in their particular home; staff need to be able to practise independently and confidently.

We were able to discern aspects of theories of leadership that were applicable, if not directly transferable, to the functional group contained in a children's home. It is not the task of this chapter to attempt to review the burgeoning academic and journalistic fields of leadership theory, study and commentary, or the corresponding volumes relating to power and influence. Literature relating to the concept of leadership and both its measurement and value is vast. We do not have to look very far to encounter over a 100 definitions of leadership alone (Burns 1978). It will be useful, however, to indicate albeit rather broadly the theoretical context against which our analyses are set before building on this literature in relation to children's homes.

Quests for the essential traits of strong leaders take the form of identifying specific qualities as demonstrated by particular figures, only recently including women, in historical or political terms (Burns 1978; Leigh and Walters 1998). Parallel quests, popular in the early to mid-20th century and resurfacing periodically since, have strived to determine essential behaviours and patterns of behaviour (Katz, Maccoby and Morse 1950; Likert 1961). These have given rise to emphasis being placed on contextual factors and the ways in which contingencies determine behaviour, and in particular the highly influential approach identified as 'situational leadership' by Hersey and Blanchard (1988). In the latter, leadership is identified as varying along the two dimensions of 'task behaviour' and 'relationship behaviour', with varying degrees of direction/delegation and limited communication/facilitating coming into play.

There is no universal agreement on the appropriateness of different management styles, although few would scorn the value of a participative stance. Theories of leadership which have been more contemporarily influential relate to transactional and transformational leaders, where the former rely upon bargaining relationships and the latter upon motivating people to go above and beyond their apparent duties (Burns 1978), and notions of dispersed leadership, where leadership is held at many levels of an organisation (Bennis and Nanus 1985). Concepts of transformational or 'new leadership', which bring together theories of style, personality and context in terms of inspiring others to high attainment, more broadly fit with the loosely defined notion of the learning organisation that reflects on its own experience in order to develop (Argyris and Schon 1978; Daft and Huber 1987; Easterby-Smith, Burgoyne and Araujo 1999; Senge 1990).

Bearing in mind these limitations, it behoves us here to focus on some of the components of leadership that are useful in helping us to consider the activity of managing children's homes in an efficient and effective manner. The following quotation provides a clear and helpful starting point for this discussion:

> If there is a clear distinction between the process of managing and the process of leading, it is in the distinction between getting others to do and getting others to want to do. Managers, we believe, get other people to do, but leaders get other people to want to do. Leaders do this by first of all being credible. They establish this credibility by their actions – by challenging, inspiring, enabling, modelling and encouraging. (Kouzes and Posner 1987, p.27)

This kind of separation of the two processes of managing and leading is frequently encountered in literature that focuses on organisational behaviour. It emphasises the motivating force that leaders come to represent, and uses a vocabulary that is in line with our description of the tasks of children's homes managers – i.e. it distinguishes the leader's role as one of motivating, coaching, educating and facilitating others' work. Other strands of thought have been less categorical in their representation of the distinction between the two realms of leader and manager (Mintzberg 1977), noting that the boundaries between the two are less distinct and that, in practice, the roles of manager and leader are not always easy to distinguish. Again, our descriptions of children's homes managers' roles would support this thinking.

Perhaps the most helpful arena for debate about people-centred leadership is that provided by the national and international literature concerned with school management. Here, leadership is seen as integrally linked to attainment outcomes (Bush and Jackson 2002; Hallinger and Heck 1999; Mortimore *et al.* 2000). Successful leaders are seen to set direction as well as model values and practices (Sergiovanni 1995). Programmes established in England by the Teacher Training Agency, such as the Headteachers'

Leadership and Management Programme (HEADLAMP), the Leadership Programme for Serving Headteachers (LPSH) and the National Professional Qualification for Headship (NPQH), although not explicitly research-oriented, are based on the conviction that effective strategic leadership can be developed through training. Important here is a complex evidence base which emphasises personal values, the monitoring of standards and the idea of being oriented towards improvement through collaboration and professional development (Sammons, Thomas and Mortimore 1997; Teddlie and Reynolds 2000).

As Gronn (1999) shows, the performance of any leader newly in post is highly influenced by the dynamics of a range of different parties and constraints prior to taking up post. Following on from this, there is considerable evidence concerned with the ways in which leadership is distributed in educational organisations that are defined as effective (Bush and Jackson 2002). The notion of the value of shared leadership and the positive conditions for this are strongly evident in the field of education. Here the interdependency of leader and team, and the associated risks of empowerment leading to poor results, is debated (Blase and Anderson 1995; Marsick and Watkins 1990; Starratt 1995). Each of these strands of thought has bearings on our work with children's homes.

What were the main approaches used by children's homes managers?

The theoretical literature on leadership can provide useful inputs. It cannot be assumed automatically that it applies directly to children's homes. Much of the literature concentrates on leadership in contexts that might be characterised as clearly delineated, often large, hierarchical organisations focused on standards and goal attainment, where different levels of performance can be identified and measured. Although these characteristics may be transferred to smaller organisations, children's homes are formed around establishing and developing caring relationships for individual children and young people within a group setting. Fluency 'in the language of emotions' is a requirement (Ward 2007). Children's homes are not engaged in tasks which result in quantifiable 'products'. The current study captures directly the experiences of those involved, in order to portray the ways that leadership is formed and distributed within these small, development and relationship focused organisations. Existing management and leadership literature has not been developed from within this context.

In practice, the literature illuminates much of what takes place. It was the case that most managers in our sample were trying to work towards establishing a collaborative approach in their work with staff teams. Most had moved away, or were in the process of moving away, from a directly participative stance in the light of their more strategic roles, although all usually found some way to model practice in order to demonstrate manner, pace and expectations.

The overall aim of managers was to achieve a working consensus among the staff team, where goals were shared and staff were equally motivated. For most, extensive sharing and equality of contribution were part of their overall value base, aim and commitment. The extent to which managers were able to bring about a collaborative approach was largely dependent on the balance they wanted or were able to achieve between retaining formal and informal responsibility for themselves, and actively empowering staff. Achieving the goal of empowering staff related largely to factors internal to the team, mainly: differences in motivation and contribution within the staff team or between the manager and the majority of the staff team; the extent to which the manager, in role, was accepted by the staff team; the extent to which goals were shared; and the extent to which collaboration and co-ordinated practice was possible. Sharing responsibilities throughout the staff team was dependent on the extent to which empowerment was possible. Delegation of tasks was deemed only possible in situations where staff were empowered – that is, where managers were assured of unity in skills, approaches and goals.

Work towards such collaborative conditions for practice took time to bring to fruition. Ultimately, what prevented collaborative sharing from occurring would mostly arise from factors beyond the immediate control of, or pre-dating in some way, the individual manager – for example, inappropriate staff appointments, or reliance on agency staff. While a collaborative approach was the overall desired goal in this setting, we did see other approaches holding sway and, most importantly, these were subject to change over time.

Building on work led by Wallace and carried out with senior management teams in large primary schools (Wallace 2001, see p.164 in particular; Wallace and Huckman 1996, 1999), we have formed an empirically derived framework for cohesive management in children's homes, as shown in Figure 6.1. The framework allows for movement *between* cells over time – that is, it allows for shifts in levels of cohesion, consistency and motivation among and between managers and their teams.

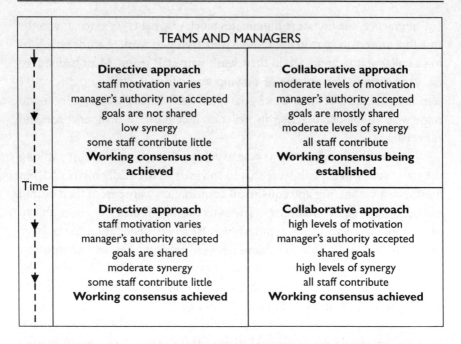

TEAMS AND MANAGERS	
Directive approach staff motivation varies manager's authority not accepted goals are not shared low synergy some staff contribute little **Working consensus not achieved**	**Collaborative approach** moderate levels of motivation manager's authority accepted goals are mostly shared moderate levels of synergy all staff contribute **Working consensus being established**
Directive approach staff motivation varies manager's authority accepted goals are shared moderate synergy some staff contribute little **Working consensus achieved**	**Collaborative approach** high levels of motivation manager's authority accepted shared goals high levels of synergy all staff contribute **Working consensus achieved**

(Time axis on left)

Figure 6.1 Children's homes staff teams and their managers: ways of working

These formulations are not to be thought of as a natural progression based on the manager's time in post or levels of experience. When situations arose where agreement was difficult to achieve, some managers asserted their authority unequivocally. Other managers were always reluctant to take a directive stance. Some were happy to begin with a tight rein and become mellow over time and with familiarity with their context for work.

Of primary importance was achieving a team dynamic that worked consistently, over time, and was able to operate within the manager's preferred approach. This was a necessary pre-requisite to putting in place correspondingly consistent, goal-oriented ways of working with young people's social, emotional and educational development. In this way, managers of children's homes spent much of their time coaching, educating and developing their teams, bringing about awareness of young people's needs and ways of working with these, and ensuring that consistency was achieved.

These tasks require high levels of skill in arenas which transcend direct management tasks associated with organisation, provision and human resources. They also require an intensive and intimate insight into day-to-day practice and the ability to act as a role model. Furthermore, they require a confident perception of the overall direction of the home in relation to its sister homes and more broadly in terms of the parent organisation. It is our contention that children's homes managers inevitably must function as leaders within their homes in order to bring about effective work with young people. A theory of leadership appropriate to children's homes must take account of the developmental nature of the manager's role – the manager is in a different position at different times – and the fluctuating nature of homes, as shown in Chapter 3.

What were the main levels of influence in managing children's homes?

Building on previous work (Ward 2007; Whitaker *et al.* 1998), we have been concerned to discriminate between levels of influence from differing sources in order to see the importance that each has to functioning as a manager of a children's home. Thus we have been able to show the ways in which homes are managed, taking into account the context for work, the ways that leadership is held and shared within teams and between teams and their managers, and the influence that each of these has on potential for practice and its management.

In terms of the parent organisation of which each home was a part, we saw differences in the way external management was described, as well as in the structure and influence of overall organisations. These we designated broadly as the 'external context'. We also saw differences in the ways individual managers described their way of working, such as their skills and knowledge, their approach and their experience base. These we identified as factors relating to the 'individual manager'. 'Home' factors related to staff and the ways in that they worked together in teams, including positive strategies for working with young people. Most importantly, we have been concerned also to show the contribution which these things make to overall outcomes for young people. Figure 6.2 shows diagrammatically these levels of functioning.

Vital to these levels of operation were the relationships established between them. Each set of relationships was interdependent. Each was held together as part of a mutually developed process. Managers felt responsibility for forming these relationships successfully; it is important to note that their awareness of their need to act as initiators was high throughout.

At the external level, we saw differences in organisational structures and ways of operating, and in relationships with the wider organisation, such as other homes. At the level of the home, we were able to see differences in many areas between and within homes, such as: the way labour was divided, shared

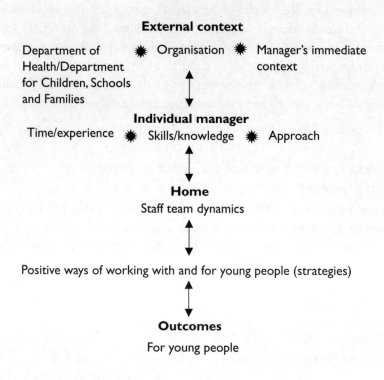

Figure 6.2 Interdependent work contexts and outcomes

and delegated; the ways that work was allocated; in values, interests and per-sonalities of the staff concerned; in the resources at the disposal of managers and staff; in managers' and staff members' ways of working; and in the ways decisions were arrived at. For managers themselves, as reported in earlier chapters, we saw crucial distinctions in their skills, knowledge and personal characteristics, in approaches to particular situations and to the work overall, and in experience and length of time in post.

The nature of influence between levels of operation potentially varied according to each home. As shown in Chapter 4, some relationships between homes and their environments permitted greater variation and thus were less determinative than others. A theory of leadership for children's homes must include the interrelationship between levels internal to the home and those external to it.

Where do differences lie in the execution of the task of managing children's homes?

The descriptive accounts were subjected to two levels of analysis. As is most usually the case with qualitative material, we undertook a thematic content analysis of the data. We then moved on to use this in conjunction with the ratings made immediately after the interviews. These were ratings of the 35 practice arenas on which the schedule was based.

Combining these two analyses enabled us to make a grounded analysis of the key areas of importance in relation to leading and managing teams successfully. This in turn enabled us to formulate an overall conception of where the 'points of bite' lay in managing homes – that is to say, the factors essential to attaining overall direction of children's homes. For this conceptual analysis we derived eight ratings and one nominal category. The ratings themselves have been taken into the statistical analyses, as will be shown in Chapters 7 and 8. The categorisations are shown in Figure 6.3, and a summary of what each entails is provided here. It will be clear that ratings for each category entailed influences from differing sources and differing levels. It is important to note that the ratings were made without awareness of the findings about the views of staff or young people and without awareness of the findings about the young people's behaviour.

External	• status of post
	• clarity in own role/purpose and function
	• time able to spend within the unit
	• autonomy
	• external support
Internal	• experience with team
	• embodies high influence on practice
	• effective strategy for behaviour
	• effective strategy for education

Figure 6.3 Characteristics contributing to facilitating leadership in children's homes

Readers will note that each of these characteristics has been described in the preceding chapters concerned with ways of managing homes. Here, we render them as separate characteristics, and briefly discuss the extent to which variation was encountered across the sample. A theory of leadership in relation to children's homes must include the ways that managers choose to exercise their roles.

What were the characteristics we discerned which contributed to the way leadership is formed in children's homes?

Characteristics external to the home

STATUS OF POST

This was a nominal categorisation. We made a simple categorisation here mainly due to the relatively small overall numbers in this part of the study. For this part of the analysis, we only noted whether or not posts were permanent.

Many combinations of posts existed within the sample. These included, for example, situations where managers acted temporarily for one home while permanently managing another, were appointed as 'acting temporary' on a week-by-week basis for one home only, or were 'acting temporary' for an identified time-limited period. In some instances managers were permanently managing two homes or more. These kinds of position were reflected in the accounts given by those who at the time of interview were in permanent posts – that is to say, it was frequently the case that managers came into role in posts where they were not able to take full authority within the home, but were expected to take full responsibility by the organisation and by staff working in the home. In such situations, uncertainty as to the extent to which a manager could fully adopt their role was commonly matched by ambivalent staff responses, disunity and inconsistencies in practice. Most usually this meant that managers had to focus extensively on establishing their own credibility, building trust and demonstrating their ability to listen to staff, and being seen to be fair to them and their interests, as individuals and as a group.

The status of the contracted post made a tangible difference to what could be achieved.

CLARITY IN OWN ROLE AND IN THE PURPOSE AND FUNCTION OF THE HOME

This was experienced to varying degrees across the sample, and was largely dependent on the way the manager's relationship with their own organisation functioned and was established over time. Variations in relationships with external managers influenced clarity or lack of it in this respect. The main reasons for variation included the following:

- the manager's understanding of how long they were expected to be in post

- whether or not the manager felt secure in or happy with the nature of the post
- the degree of ownership managers experienced or claimed for themselves
- clarity on the organisational aims for the home itself – that is, holding a clear and detailed brief about what the home was supposed to do and achieve, and the time frame around this
- whether any changes were planned, and the reliability of information about this
- perceptions of organisational expectations in relation to the direction the home should be taking
- the extent to which all parties concerned adhered to the stated purpose and function of the home.

TIME ABLE TO SPEND WITHIN THE UNIT

This was considered an essential part of keeping in touch with the home, and something for which to aim. Many managers felt they were unable to spend enough time within the home, due to varying circumstances, usually beyond their control. Functioning at a strategic level within the organisation was regarded as beneficial to the home and to the nature of the overall service provided, because it enabled managers to contribute to organisational aims. This did, however, mean that managers frequently found themselves with insufficient time available to spend in their home. Managers had to retain flexibility about the amount of extra time they were able to contribute to the home as a result. The amount of formal and informal time a manager was able to spend working within their home varied according to:

- the function of the manager within the wider organisation
- organisational expectations and requirements
- the individual needs and approach of the manager
- domestic circumstances
- the climate of the home at given points.

Most managers expected to contribute their own time to the running of the unit; the extent to which they were able to do this varied according to their personal circumstances, which changed over time. Sometimes living at a distance from the home was seen to be disadvantageous in providing the kinds of immediate support which from time to time was seen as essential –

sometimes living nearby was seen to be disadvantageous in terms of being called upon too frequently.

AUTONOMY

The extent to which autonomous work was achieved varied largely according to the perceived expectations of the parent organisation in relation to the skills, experience and personal qualities of the manager. The main points of variation can be accounted for in terms of:

- the formal and informal status which the manager experienced within their organisation
- the manager's experience in residential child care or in management posts
- the structure of the parent organisation
- the nature of the task with which the manager was charged
- the climate of the home itself
- future plans for the home.

The ways that homes were managed in respect of rotas being drawn up and allocated depended on the structure of the organisation. Where organisations and homes were small, rotas were often written and allocated centrally. Smaller homes usually worked with a consistently high ratio of staff to young people come what may. In larger organisations, the structuring of rotas and the allocation of staff were usually matters for individual homes to manage. In the latter case, it was both necessary and possible to vary staff time according to the daily needs of young people as individuals and as a group.

Jurisdiction in terms of autonomous working often left managers with a particular and recurrent problem in the week-by-week running of homes – namely, the use of staff time off in lieu (referred to most usually, in this and other contexts, as 'TOIL'). This often amassed to such an extent that it became impossible to take time off that corresponded to the numbers of hours owed without producing further displacement of staff hours. This local negotiation of additional resourcing would at times get out of hand for managers, producing disharmony among the staff group, which in turn increased stressors within the home. Ultimately, where no apparently fair agreement could be reached about time owed, staff would take sick leave in order to retrieve time given in goodwill. This kind of strained spiralling could only be contained locally for a limited period, and once drawn to the attention of senior managers would become evidence of poor functioning. In some situations, managers of children's homes were able to build a case for additional permanent staffing thereby reducing unpredictable increases in staff time, but these situations rarely came to fruition. Cases were most likely to be successful if practice was deemed good and outcomes judged by the organisation as consistently positive.

EXTERNAL SUPPORT

As noted previously, external support offered to managers varied in both frequency and kind, and was linked to the nature of the relationship formed with line managers. Main reasons for variation included:

- the manager's formal and informal status within the organisation
- the climate of the home
- the extent to which managers felt the need for, or thought it appropriate to draw upon, support
- the extent to which changes for the home were occurring
- perceptions of the respective line manager's views about the direct manager's ability
- organisational requirements and the role of the line manager.

Most support was provided when homes were in crisis. Often supervision was forgone if the home was ticking over well or line managers were busy in other arenas. The nature of support varied – phone as and when needed, calling in, email, formal arrangements with agendas. The frequency and form of external support usually depended on the nature of the relationship between manager and external manager. Where trust and mutual respect were present, supervision was thought of as valuable, if not always necessary. The exact nature of supervision varied widely, with few examples of planned and agreed procedures encountered across the sample.

Characteristics internal to the home
EXPERIENCE WITH THE TEAM

This entailed the extent to which managers were able to enculture their teams overall into their approach, and thereby felt able to rely upon them to know and understand how to operate. This category applied most positively to homes that had structures for practice and its management in place, and where staff were thought to work cohesively, consistently, resiliently and with commitment to the manager, young people and to the job itself. In homes with the highest scores here, the manager would be seen to think of the team as their own in some fashion – that is, as 'my team'. Main reasons for variation included:

- the manager's type of experience with the team and with individual members of staff (e.g. duration of experience together, nature of the initial appointment, extent of shared adversities/conflicts, nature of relationships)

- the manager's experience in residential child care

- perceptions about the stability of the team

- perceptions of the team's shared sense of purpose, belonging and achievement

- the extent to which the manager felt confident within the parent organisation.

EMBODIES HIGH INFLUENCE ON PRACTICE

This entailed the manager being strong on educating and developing staff, and on leading by example and showing the way. In some situations, those occupying other roles held a greater degree of influence from time to time. Main points of variation included:

- the nature of the staff team

- the extent to which the team were thought to look to the manager for practice direction and ways of operating

- the duration of shared working experience – that is, the manager and staff being in post together

- the manager's own experience

- the extent to which the manager 'held' the home and played an active part as distinct from being a reference point

- the perceived influence of other members of staff, or the organisation itself, in relation to that of the manager

- the history of the home

- the extent to which taking time for supervision formed a part of the culture of the home.

Where managers held high influence, they had spent considerable time on educating individual members of staff and the staff team about their practice, putting in place their preferred way of operating, and maintaining preferred approaches.

EFFECTIVE STRATEGY FOR BEHAVIOUR

This entailed issues of control and ways for working with particular kinds of behaviour being clearly understood as part of the culture of the home, such that staff were perceived as sufficiently confident and competent in working with complex behaviours in a unified manner. Variation was encountered with respect to:

- negotiation of consistent and realistic boundaries
- the ways in which troubled behaviour was defined, and how problematic this was seen to be overall
- the extent to which this was seen as a priority with which to get to grips
- perceptions of the experience, stability and capability of staff team
- the duration and nature of the shared working experience – i.e. the manager and staff being in post together
- the utilisation of token economies.

Here it was important that the manager knew what to do next if things were not working out, and which networks to involve when and where necessary. It was also important that managers were able to bring about the next steps with young people through their staff teams. In order to do this they had to be able to rely on staff to function in accordance with a considered and identifiable approach.

EFFECTIVE STRATEGY FOR EDUCATION

This was similar in principle to the 'effective strategy for behaviour' category outlined earlier. In practice, this entailed creating and maintaining relationships across the boundary of the home much more intensively than did the 'behaviour and control' arena of practice. This category entailed bringing about clearly defined ways of working with young people and professionals (for example, in respect of establishing and maintaining their education, getting them to school where appropriate and keeping them there in a positive manner). Much of practice in this respect entailed working with other professionals, usually educationalists, to convince them of the merits of the young people in their care and help them to understand ways of working with them from within an educational setting.

Variation occurred in relation to:

- the expectations of the home itself
- the expectations of the parent organisation

- the extent to which education per se was prioritised and seen as valuable
- perceptions of the experience, stability and capability of the staff team
- the duration and nature of the shared working experience – i.e. the manager and staff being in post together
- the resourcing of staff time for external activities, including providing support within schools.

Implications of distinguishing between characteristics contributing to the way leadership is formed in children's homes

From the detailed descriptions of tasks we elicited during the course of the qualitative part of this project, we have arrived at a conceptualisation of the areas which matter in getting to grips with the challenge of managing a children's home and in coming to own the task in a thoroughgoing way.

We have intended to show that successful execution of the task is dependent upon factors that sit in dynamic relationship with each other, drawn from different contexts. We have emphasised the importance of the influence which the manager exerts in terms of the internal and external contexts in which they operate. Interdependent arenas include individual managers' approaches within the home, with the staff group, with the group of young people, together with approaches in contextual arenas such as the organisation, other agencies, and the wider realm of policy and procedures. The overall potential of managers relies on them being sufficiently well placed within each of these arenas to bring about consistent and reflective practice for and on behalf of the young people living in the care of the home itself.

In combination, ways of working with staff teams, levels of functioning internal and external to the home, and ways of working with young people are important aspects of overall leadership, as illuminated by extensive literature. We have intended to show that the accumulation of strengths in different arenas acts as an overall enabler of good practice. It remains for us now to explore the mutual relationship between these varying characteristics, the way residential child care is resourced, and the results which it is able to bring about.

Summary

This chapter brings together our qualitative analysis of the roles of children's homes managers in terms of a conceptualisation of leadership. Drawing on a wide body of literature relating to leadership within organisations, we link dimensions of the role to the ways in which leadership is formed within homes over time.

Our conceptualisation of leadership as it relates to children's homes takes account of three main components: the developmental nature of the manager's role; the interrelationship between what occurs in the home itself and what occurs in the external context; and the way the role is exercised. Achieving a team dynamic, which works consistently over time and utilises the manager's preferred approach, is of key importance. This is essential to establishing consistency in ways of working with young people. The chapter examines the approaches used and the ways of working that are established between teams and managers within the fluctuating nature of homes. Further to this, we consider interdependent levels of functioning and the internal and external levels of influence that come to bear on the way the role is performed within the organisational context.

The detailed analysis used in this part of the research provided ratings for key areas of importance in relation to managing children's homes, thereby allowing us to discriminate between being able to perform the role of manager adequately and being able to perform the role well. As will be seen, the ratings described in the later sections of this chapter are taken forward into the statistical analyses in Chapters 7 and 8.

The following chapter continues our exploration of the dimensions of variance in the way children's homes function by focusing on resources, their costs and their relationship to outcomes. Readers may recall from Chapter 1 that this is an important component of the study. Thus Chapter 7 provides a detailed economic exploration of variations between residential homes for children and young people. Of necessity, Chapter 7 contains technical information that we know will be of particular interest to specific audiences. For those who are less concerned with such detail, we have provided narratives for each table and, as in other chapters, a summary of the main findings.

What Resources Are Used, How Much Do These Cost, and How Are Costs Linked to Outcomes?

Introduction

One of the aims of the study was to explore the cost-effectiveness of residential care for children and young people. Previous studies of children's social care services rarely include an economic component (Beecham and Sinclair 2007). However, the increasing demands that have been placed on these services have heightened the need to assess value for money. There is now considerable interest in obtaining evidence to inform how best to use available resources 1. across different types of social services and 2. for different ways of delivering the same services. Typically, economic evaluation involves comparing the costs and outcomes of competing services in order to identify which produce the greatest benefit for the resources invested (Drummond *et al.* 2005). This chapter provides a first step to understanding the economics of children's homes.

As discussed in Chapter 1, residential care for children has been fraught with difficulties in recent years, and a key issue has been the expense associated with providing this form of care. In 2000 it was estimated that residential care for young people in England alone cost £735 million. This expenditure exceeded that spent on foster care even though the total number of resident weeks for young people in foster care was five times higher (CIPFA 2002). Although dramatic, such facts do not provide any information on the appropriateness of these variations or how this investment is linked to outputs for young people in residential care.

There has been some discussion in the literature about the diverse use made of resources and the variation in the costs of children's homes (Carr-Hill *et al.* 1997; Hughes 1988; Knapp *et al.* 1990). Little evidence exists, however, to explain why the cost of homes varies. Some of this variation may be explained by the substantial diversity often reported in the characteristics of young people in residential care (Brown *et al.* 1998; Gibbs and Sinclair 1999; Sinclair and Gibbs 1998a, 1998b), or by more practical issues of supply, such as the location of the home or the provision of in-house education. This chapter explores such hypotheses in order to gain a better understanding of factors associated with variation in costs of children's homes and the appropriateness of this variation from a policy perspective.

Also of importance in assessing the management and delivery of residential care is the relationship between inputs, including services supplied to children in residential care, and outputs, including young people's outcomes. There is considerable uncertainty about what constitutes a successful children's home and under what circumstances residential care offers the best value for money. This chapter explores factors which influence good outcomes – for example, whether resources and characteristics of managers of homes are important factors, or whether other factors, such as the characteristics of young people, are more important. To this end, secondary analyses explore the factors that influence good outcomes, in an attempt to determine characteristics that make for a successful home.

Finally, a tentative exploration of the relative cost-effectiveness of local authority and non-statutory sector homes was undertaken. The literature on this is not clear-cut. Anecdotally, there has been a general perception that private sector homes are more expensive than local authority provision. However, Knapp (1987) found that, at the time of writing, non-statutory sector fees were in fact lower than local authority costs, even after standardisation. Similarly, more recent figures for the financial year 1999–2000 show that the average standard charge per resident per week for local authority provision in Great Britain is higher than for other provision (including non-statutory sector homes and provision by other local authorities) (CIPFA 2000). This section explores the relative cost of alternative sector delivery of residential care, attempts to explain any differences found and tries to relate cost differences to differences in outcomes.

Methods

The aims of the economic analysis were to explore:

1. factors that influence the cost of children's homes per resident per week

2. factors that influence the general well-being of residents

3. the incremental difference in mean costs and effects associated with local authority compared to non-statutory sector provision of residential care.

Given the difficulty of allocating residential care resources on the basis of individual use, the cost of the homes in this study were calculated at the level of the home, rather than the individual. As a secondary analysis, the individual use and cost of services external to the home were also estimated, including health, education, voluntary, private sector and youth justice services. These broader costs are relevant because it is likely that they will influence, and be influenced by, the resources provided within the homes. For example, the cost of one home might be relatively high in comparison to another home, but, if it was more successful at generating good outcomes, the residents' use of services outside the home may be lower, resulting in lower total costs of care packages.

Economic data collection and unit cost estimation

Standard costing methodologies were applied to estimate costs in this study (Allen and Beecham 1993). This involves identification of services and resources relevant to the population of interest, identification of the unit of measurement for each service or resource, measurement of the quantities of each services or resource used and calculation of the unit costs (Allen and Beecham 1993). All cost figures relate to 2001–2002 prices, reflecting the data collection period. Any costs collected from earlier financial years were adjusted to 2001–2002 prices using the personal social services price indices (Curtis and Netten 2006). While these costs are appropriate for the data collection period, costs will clearly have risen since the study was undertaken. To give an indication of the impact of inflation on these costs in the intervening years, the inflation indices in Table 7.1 can be applied:

Table 7.1 Inflation indices – retail price

Year	Index (1986/1987 = 100)	% increase
2002	177.6	3.2
2003	182.6	2.8
2004	188.1	3.1
2005	193.1	2.7

Source: Data drawn from Curtis and Netten (2006).

Data on the cost of homes and the use of external services were collected using questionnaires sent to each manager and/or finance officer of the 45 homes participating in the study.

Cost of residential care

Data necessary to calculate the annual cost of the children's homes were collected using a questionnaire designed by Berridge *et al.* (2002). The questionnaire that was used to calculate the costs of homes asked for information on the total annual recurrent costs of the children's homes, capital costs, and the current and maximum number of residents in the homes. The total annual recurrent cost of a home is the yearly cost of operating the facility and includes such things as management costs, insurance payments, staff costs and the cost of consumables such as heating, lighting and transport. Capital costs are the stock of assets that are capable of generating an income, such as buildings.

Management costs were not always reported and instead were imputed on the basis of the proportion of total annual recurrent costs that management costs accounted for in homes where such information was provided. The calculation was performed separately for local authority and non-statutory sector homes to take into consideration the possibility that management costs may differ significantly across sectors. Mean imputed management costs were 10.6% of total annual recurrent costs for local authority homes and 6.4% for non-statutory sector homes.

The economic costs of capital buildings were calculated using information provided by the Building Cost Information Service (BCIS) website (www.bcis.co.uk). Calculations were based on the current rebuild value of the home and assumed that residential care took place in a medium-sized, detached house. In practice, as we have discussed in Chapter 2, residential care was provided in a diverse range of buildings from terraced accommodation to large, detached houses.

Calculations for each home were based on the region where the home was located and the age of the home. If the age of the building was not known, it was assumed to be modern (built in 1980 or after) because rebuild costs of modern properties are lower per metre squared than older properties and therefore a more conservative estimate is obtained. The annual cost of each home was calculated by annuitising the current rebuild value of the home over a 60-year period, assumed to be equivalent to the useful life of a building. The annuitised cost (cost per year) was estimated on the basis of the amount that would have to be paid during each year of the useful life of the home in order to repay an equivalent amount of money loaned to rebuild the property plus interest on the loan. The interest rate was assumed to be 5 per cent. The formula used to annuitize capital costs can be found in Hunink *et al.* (2001).

The total cost of each home was converted into a cost per resident per week on the basis of the total number of current residents in the home at the time of initial data collection (T1).

Cost of other services

Data on the use of other services used by residents outside the home were recorded using a second questionnaire designed for the purpose of the study and based on one developed for an earlier study involving children and young people (Byford *et al.* 1999). Residents' use of services external to the homes was recorded for the previous three months since service use over a longer time frame becomes increasingly difficult to recall and there was a concern not to overburden respondents. For education, managers of homes were asked to record the type of school attended by each current resident over the previous week. If the residents were on school holidays, then school attendance was recorded for the last week of the previous school term.

Table 7.2 lists the types of external services used by children in the study and reports the unit costs applied to each service and the source of the unit cost data. Unit costs of hospital services were gathered from trust financial returns (CIPFA 2001). Unit costs of community health services and social services, including field social workers, leaving care workers and family support workers, were sourced from nationally applicable unit costs (Netten, Rees and Harrison 2001). The cost of mainstream primary and secondary schools and all special schools attended (including pupil referral units and learning support units) were calculated using CIPFA (2000) data and related to the schools in the residential home locality. A small number of residents received home tuition and these costs were estimated using the methodology reported by Berridge *et al.* (2002). The mid-point of the pay scale for qualified teachers was used, including employers' National Insurance and Super-annuation contributions. A percentage (65%) was added to cover 'other institutional' expenditure and local education authority (LEA) overheads. Unit costs of police contacts and youth custody were those calculated by Finn, Hyslop and Truman (2000).

The cost of all the services that were used, external to the residential homes, were summed and added to the cost of the homes. A cost per resident per week was then calculated on the basis of the total number of current residents in the home at initial data collection (T1).

Outcome measures

Outcomes were assessed at the initial time point (T1) and about a year later (T2) using postal questionnaires sent to all residents of the homes participating in the study. The primary outcome measure for the economic evaluation was the general well-being section of the *Lancashire Quality of Life (LQOL) Profile* (Oliver *et al.* 1996, 1997) previously referred to in Chapter 2. This is an *end outcome*, focusing on the individual, and is generally preferred for use in economic evaluations, compared to *intermediate outcomes*, such as educational qualifications, or *process* measures, which are focused more on issues of service provision, such as days in residential care (Sefton *et al.* 2002). Although the *LQOL Profile* is more commonly employed in mental health populations (Huxley *et al.* 2001), standardised measures of quality of life are not commonly available in social care and the general well-being section of this profile is not specific to any one type of population, being a measure of general happiness.

The primary element of the general well-being section is based on Cantril's ladder (Cantril 1965), and developed by Oliver *et al.* (1996). It may be recalled from Chapter 2 that respondents are asked to place a mark on the ladder to indicate how they feel their life is at the moment, given that the top of the ladder represents life 'when things couldn't be better' and the bottom of the ladder represents life 'when things couldn't be worse'. The ladder produces a 0–100 point continuous scale, zero representing the worst outcome and 100 representing the best outcome.

Table 7.2 Unit costs of services used outside the children's home

Services	Unit cost or range (£)	Source of unit cost
Hospital services		
Inpatient, psychiatric night	354.82	CIPFA (2001)
Inpatient, medical night	393.19	CIPFA (2001)
Outpatient, psychiatric attendance	216.98	CIPFA (2001)
Outpatient, medical attendance	112.33	CIPFA (2001)
Accident and emergency attendance	51.33	CIPFA (2001)
Community health services		
GP surgery attendance	15.51	Netten et al. (2001)
GP home visit per minute	2.32	Netten et al. (2001)
Dentist attendance	5.00	NHS charge
Social services		
Social worker hour of client related activity	26.25	Netten et al. (2001)
Leaving care worker hour of client related activity	26.25	Netten et al. (2001)
Family support worker hour of client related activity	28.08	Netten et al. (2001)
Education services		
Education welfare officer hour of client related activity	26.25	Netten et al. (2001)
School nurse half hour attendance	13.52	Netten et al. (2001)
Home tuition hour	31.00	Berridge et al. (2002)
Schools		
Mainstream per year	2683–3206	CIPFA (2000)
Special school per year	11,969–26,917	CIPFA (2000)
Youth justice		
Police 15-minute contact	13.44	Finn et al. (2000)
Youth custody/prison per hour	28.72	Finn et al. (2000)
Private sector services		
Optician attendance	15.00	Standard charge
Therapist attendance	15.00	Standard charge

Data analysis
Analysis of cost

To explore what influences the cost of homes, two multiple regression analyses (cost-function analyses) were undertaken using ordinary least squares (OLS) regression. OLS is the most extensively used method of regression analysis, and it is used to estimate the strength of a modelled relationship between one or more dependent variables and the independent variable. The main regression analysis explored which baseline variables were associated with variation in the average cost of each home per resident per week. The secondary regression explored which baseline variables were associated with variation in the average cost of each home plus external services used outside the home per resident per week.

Before undertaking the regression analysis, univariate associations between cost and each of the independent variables were investigated. For the continuous variables results are presented split at the median; however, the continuous data were analysed using simple linear regression. For categorical variables, one-way analysis of variance was used.

Multiple regression was used to reduce the variable set to those independently associated with costs. Variables from the pre-specified list were selected using an approach recommended for survival data (Collett 1994). Initially, a multiple regression was fitted, which included all variables that had important univariate associations with costs. All variables that no longer contributed to the model were removed. Following this, all the variables that did not have a univariate association with cost were added back in, one at a time, and were retained if they added significantly to the model. This model was checked to ensure that no other terms added significantly to it at a level of statistical significance around 10 per cent.

Standard OLS regression methods on untransformed costs were used for the analyses even though the distribution of the cost data was positively skewed (large number of low-cost cases alongside a small number of high-cost cases, rather than a symmetrical distribution of cases). Frequently when data is skewed logarithmic transformation or non-parametric methods are applied. However, the advantage of using parametric tests is the ability to make inferences about the arithmetic mean, which is of particular importance for cost data since when summed it provides meaningful budgetary information (Barber and Thompson 1998). To be confident in the use of parametric tests, non-parametric bootstrap analysis was also undertaken to check the robustness of the confidence intervals (CIs) and p-values generated in the parametric analyses (Efron and Tibshirani 1993). Bootstrap analysis is used to simulate data and does not require assumptions about the underlying distribution of the data. Results from the analyses were also checked against the results gained from a generalised linear model (an extension of OLS regression) with a non-normal distribution assumed for costs (as the cost data are not symmetrically distributed) (Blough, Madden and Hornbrook 1999). In the generalised linear model, a gamma distribution was applied, rather than a normal distribution. Like the majority of cost data, gamma distributions are positively skewed; therefore, such models might be expected to provide a better fit.

Analyses were conducted on the basis of a statistical plan drawn up prior to analysis of the data, which followed the methods specified in Byford, Barber and Harrington (2001). The variables that were included in the cost-function analyses were chosen by members of the research team, on the premise that such factors were likely to be associated with costs. These pre-specified variables were collected at T1 from the *Questionnaire to Young People*, the *Questionnaire to Social Workers*, records collected within the home, the *Resident Logs* and the ratings created from the in-depth interviews with the managers of the homes. They included:

- Age (years).
- Gender (% male).
- Residents' well-being (using Cantril's ladder from the general well-being section of the *LQOL Profile*).
- Whether some residents exhibited delinquent behaviour prior to entry to the home according to residents' social workers (Yes/No).
- 'Pressure to temptation' prior to entry to the home from the resident's point of view. This variable is based on seven questions that asked residents about possible pressures on them before they came to the home – for example, whether or not the resident had been 'offered cannabis' and various temptations and pressures they had experienced both during their time in the home and before they arrived. The scoring for each of the individual items was 0 for 'No' and 1 for 'Yes' and these were summed to provide a total score. The total score therefore ranged from a minimum of 0 to a maximum of 7 with a higher score reflecting greater temptation.
- Residents' length of stay in the home (days).
- Staff satisfaction – a variable created by summing staff responses to two questions, both of which asked about different aspects of

satisfaction with the job. Both questions scored 1 to 4 on a Likert rating scale and scores for the derived variable therefore ranged from 2 to 8. The higher the score the greater the level of satisfaction.

- Staff perception of the sufficiency of staff numbers. This was a sub-scale consisting of four items, each item seeking respondents' views about different aspects of the sufficiency of staff numbers. The individual items were scored 1 to 3 and then summed to provide a simple sub-scale score with a minimum value of 3 and a maximum of 12. The higher the score the greater the perception of sufficient staff.

- Staff to resident ratio (the number of care staff per young person).

- Occupancy rate (% of maximum occupancy).

- Use of waking night staff (Yes/No).

- Local authority or non-statutory sector.

- Whether in-house education was provided (Yes/No).

- Whether the home was located in the south of England (Yes/No).

- Manager's strategy relating to education and behaviour. This variable contains two items identified from the analysis of the interviews with managers of homes and thought likely to influence cost. The first item reflects strategies for encouraging, supporting and making sure that young people attended school, and the second item reflects strategies for promoting good and dealing with bad behaviour. The variable is a simple summation of the scores for the two strategy items.

Since a relatively small number of homes were included in the study, it was important to keep the number of independent variables used in the regression to a minimum, because each addition of a variable reduces the statistical power of the regression. At the same time it was important to choose variables that were as sensitive to variation in costs as possible. The location variable, for example, could have been categorised in a number of different ways, such as by local authority or North, South and Midlands. In order to keep the number of variables to a minimum, however, we categorised location as South of England or Other. Given the higher prices associated with the south of England, it was felt that this method of categorisation would be sufficiently accurate to predict any cost variation across homes.

Analysis of outcomes

To explore factors that influence the overall well-being of the young people, multi-level modelling was used. Multi-level modelling is a statistical technique that allows analysis of the variability in the response variable selected at each level, after taking into account the selected independent variables (Rice and Jones 1997).

The method is frequently used to examine health services and educational settings by looking at all hierarchical levels in the population concerned. For example, in a school environment it may be assumed that a student's performance in examination will depend on factors at a number of different levels. Some of these, such as intelligence quotient (IQ), will have to do with the pupils themselves (level 1). Others will have to do with the class of which the pupil is part – for example, the skill of the class teacher (level 2). Yet others will have to do with the school itself (level 3). Multi-level modelling assists in explaining student performance in terms of variables at these different levels. Generally it is suitable for use in most situations where individuals are 'nested' within units that may in turn be nested within others (for examples see Goldstein and Sammons 1997; Leyland and Goldstein 2001).

In the context of children's homes, the variability in the dependent variable (based on the individual level data) may be broken down into 1. variability across young people within homes and 2. variability across homes. Multi-level analysis is used to explore the contribution of independent variables to explaining these two sources of variability.

The software package MLwiN was used to undertake the multi-level modelling (Rasbash *et al.* 2004). As in other forms of regression, the dependent variable is regressed against a set of pre-specified independent baseline variables. The dependent variable chosen was the general well-being score (Cantril's ladder) from the *LQOL Profile* (Oliver *et al.* 1996, 1997). The pre-specified independent variables, collected at T1 from the *Questionnaire to Young People*, the *Questionnaire to Social Workers*, the *Details of Home Questionnaire*, the *Resident Logs* and the ratings created from the in-depth interviews with the managers of the homes, included the variables that follow. A description of the variables used and how they were derived is explained earlier in the cost analysis sub-section:

- age
- gender

- whether some residents exhibited delinquent behaviour prior to entry to the home
- pressure to temptation prior to entry to the home
- residents' length of stay in the home
- staff satisfaction
- staff perception of the sufficiency of staff numbers
- staff to resident ratio
- occupancy rate
- local authority or non-statutory sector
- manager's strategy relating to education and behaviour
- cost of home per resident per week.

The multi-level model was set up with a random intercept to explore variation in outcomes across homes. Initially, all variables were entered into the model and then, through a process of backward elimination, independent variables that were not statistically significantly related to the average well-being of young people in the homes were taken out of the model, one by one.

The most parsimonious model that used the largest number of cases and which had the greatest explanatory power was chosen.

Results

Characteristics of homes

Questionnaires on the cost of homes were returned by all 45 homes participating in the study, although not all questionnaires were complete. As shown in Table 7.3, the average number of beds available per home was just over six, although the average number of beds occupied was only five, giving an average occupancy rate of 84 per cent. Average length of stay was almost a year (326 days). Staff costs accounted for 65 per cent of the total cost of homes on average. The average value of the homes was reported to be over £300,000.

In total, the average amount the homes charged per week per resident was £1,808–£2,049 in the non-statutory sector and £1,665 in the local authority sector. These figures may differ from the cost of the home as some included a profit element and may have been estimated on the basis of expenditure in the previous year (the best available data), rather than on actual current expenditure. The difference in charges between the two sectors was statistically significant at the 10 per cent level (p=.094, CI: − 71.27 to 838.86), with the non-statutory sector being more expensive than local authority provision.

Table 7.3 Home level characteristics

	Number of homes responding	Average	Standard deviation
Maximum number of beds	45	6.22	2.31
Occupied number of beds	43	5.05	1.85
Occupancy rates	43	84%	17
Length of stay	40	326	181
Staff cost as a % of total cost of home	43	65%	11
Value of property as reported by home managers	38	£302,477	£254.120
Charge per week	35	£1,808	£605

Cost of homes

Fourteen homes (31%) provided in-house education, including two local authority sector homes and 12 non-statutory sector homes, and these costs were included in the overall cost of a children's home. Twenty-nine homes (65%) did not provide in-house education. Two homes did not state whether or not education was provided in-house.

The costs of homes in this study are given in Table 7.4. The average cost of residential care per resident per week was estimated to be £1,543 including the cost of in-house education provision, or approximately £80,000 per resident per year. There was over a five-fold variation in the cost per resident per week ranging from £622 to £3,823.

The cost of local authority homes was found to be lower on average, at £1,491 per resident per week or £77,759 per resident per year than the cost of non-statutory sector homes at £1,664 per resident per week or £86,754 per resident per year, although this difference was not statistically significant. Since non-statutory sector homes were more likely to provide in-house education (see Figure 7.1), this comparison does not compare like with like. A second comparison was therefore undertaken which excluded the cost of in-house education from the cost of the homes. As Table 7.4 shows, the difference between the two sectors disappears, with the cost of non-statutory sector

Table 7.4 Cost of homes (£)

	All homes (n=43)	Local authority provision (n=30)	Non-statutory sector provision (n=13)	
	Mean (standard deviation)			p-value
Cost per resident per week including in-house education	1,543 (697)	1,491 (607)	1,664 (888)	.531
Cost per resident per year including in-house education	80,478 (36,340)	77,759 (31,627)	86,754 (46,299)	
Cost per resident per week excluding in-house education	1,468 (654)	1,479 (598)	1,444 (794)	.875
Cost per resident per year excluding in-house education	76,544 (34,075)	77,094 (31,156)	75,276 (41,420)	

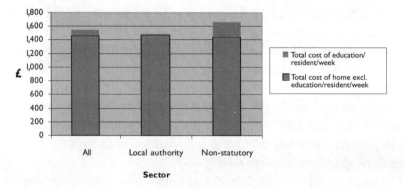

Figure 7.1 Cost of homes

homes dropping to £1,444. Thus the provision of in-house education seems to explain the difference in cost between the two sectors.

Since 26 homes (60.5%) were less than fully occupied, the costs reported earlier, based on actual occupancy levels, will differ from the cost per resident if the home were at maximum occupancy. It can be seen from Table 7.5 that the average cost per resident per week would fall if homes were operating at maximum occupancy levels, although to do so may require additional resources such as extra staff.

Table 7.5 Comparison of costs based on actual and maximum occupancy levels

	Mean (standard deviation) 2001/2002		
	All homes (n=43)	Local authority provision (n=30)	Non-statutory sector provision (n=13)
Cost per resident per week based on actual occupancy level (£)	1,543 (697)	1,494 (608)	1,669 (892)
Cost per resident per week based on maximum occupancy level (£)	1,219 (601)	1,209 (457)	1,239 (853)

UNIVARIATE ASSOCIATIONS WITH THE COST OF HOMES

Table 7.6 sets out the univariate relationships between the cost of homes per resident per week and the pre-specified independent variables. At the 5 per cent level of statistical significance, higher costs were significantly associated with a shorter length of stay by residents in the home, a higher staff to resident ratio, a lower occupancy rate and location of the home in the south, rather than elsewhere in the country. Some residents being categorised as delinquent prior to entry to the home came very close to statistical significance ($p=.053$). All these associations are in the direction that would be expected.

MULTIVARIATE ASSOCIATIONS WITH THE COST OF HOMES

The final multiple regression for the cost of homes is shown in Table 7.7. Independent variables significantly associated with home costs per resident per week in the regression included the staff to resident ratio and the location of the home. On average, costs were higher the higher the staff to resident ratio and for homes located in the south of England as compared to elsewhere. The coefficient indicates the increase in cost per unit increase in the covariate. Hence, a 1 per cent increase in the staff to resident ratio is associated with a £9 increase in the cost of homes per resident per week, on average. In terms of location, the coefficient suggests that homes in the south of England cost approximately £700 per resident per week more, on average, than homes elsewhere.

Table 7.6 Univariate associations with the cost of homes per resident per week

Independent variable	Number of homes[1]	Mean cost (SD)	p-value
Age (mean)[2]			
≤ 14.33	22	1,539 (622)	
> 14.33	21	1,548 (783)	.901
Gender (% male)[2]			
≤ 60%	23	1,667 (763)	
> 60%	20	1,402 (601)	.127
Residents' well-being[2]			
Low well-being ≤ 57.75	21	1,495 (652)	
High well-being > 57.75	21	1,573 (764)	.320
Staff satisfaction[2]			
Low staff satisfaction ≤ 42.6	22	1,516 (616)	
High staff satisfaction > 42.6	21	1,572 (787)	.952
Staff perception of sufficiency of staff[2]			
Insufficient staff ≤ 8.67	21	1,513 (654)	
Sufficient staff > 8.67	22	1,573 (750)	.764
Delinquency prior to entry to home[3]			
No residents categorised as delinquent	7	1,063 (335)	
Some residents categorised as delinquent	35	1,614 (710)	.053*
Pressure to temptation prior to entry to home[2]			
Low pressure ≤ 1.85	21	1,491 (753)	
High pressure > 1.85	21	1,577 (664)	.380
Length of stay (mean)[2]			
≤ 308 days	20	1,908 (773)	
> 308 days	19	1,196 (417)	.002*

Independent variable	Number of homes[1]	Mean cost (SD)	p-value
Staff to resident ratio[2]			
≤ 71%	22	1,142 (366)	
> 71%	20	1,957 (742)	.000*
Occupancy rate[2]			
≤ 83%	19	1,757 (666)	
> 83%	21	1,319 (701)	.018*
Waking night staff			
Yes	6	1,854 (794)	
No	37	1,493 (678)	.244
Sector			
Local authority	30	1,491 (607)	
Non-statutory	13	1,664 (888)	.463
In-house education provided			
Yes	14	1,749 (846)	
No	29	1,444 (604)	.183
Location			
South of England	11	2,281 (691)	
Other (Midlands or north of England)	32	1,290 (495)	.000*
Strategy relating to education and behaviour[2]			
Less positive strategies ≤ 7.00	18	1,701 (589)	
Positive strategies > 7.00	22	1,385 (746)	.187

Notes:
1 Some missing data.
2 Split at the median but analysed as continuous data.
3 As measured by young people's social workers.
*Statistically significant at the 10% level at least; SD = standard deviation.

Table 7.7 Multiple regression for the cost of homes

Variables	Coefficient	95% confidence interval	p-value
Staff to resident ratio	8.79	5.74 to 11.8	.000
South versus other	711	404 to 357	.000

The adjusted r^2, which reflects the amount of cost variation explained through the model, was .69 suggesting that the model was able to explain almost 70 per cent of the variation in the cost of homes within the sample. Findings from the generalised linear model with gamma distribution errors and the bootstrap regression analyses were similar to the simple linear regressions reported in the tables, and so are not reported here.

Cost of external services

Details on the use of services external to the children's home by all residents over a three-month period were obtained from 28 children's homes in the sample (62%). In addition, limited information on use of external services was gathered for an additional four homes from the cost of children's homes questionnaire, as described in the 'Cost of residential care' section above, giving a total of 34 homes that provided some data (76%).

The completion of some of the questionnaires was piecemeal and the accuracy of the data captured for this part of the study is likely to be poor, probably due to the time-consuming nature and complexity of the collection and reporting of such data. The data are likely to give a fairly good impression of the *types* of services accessed by residents outside the home setting, but accuracy in terms of the *quantity* of each service used may be more limited; thus caution should be applied when interpreting the results.

Table 7.8 details the average use of external services per resident per year, calculated by multiplying the three-month data collected by four and dividing by the number of young people in the home. Services most commonly reported to have been accessed included field social workers, leaving care workers, education welfare officers, the police and various therapists.

Table 7.9 reports the total cost of all external services by sector and the total cost of the care package provided, including the cost of homes. The cost of services that are external to the homes accounted for 7 per cent of the total costs of homes, on average. This will be an underestimate because we only asked for information on what we felt were 'key services' (services expected to be significant contributors to cost or those thought likely to be accessed by a large proportion of young people).

Table 7.8 Use of external services, mean per resident over 12 months

Service	Mean use of services (standard deviation)
Hospital services	
Inpatient psychiatry nights	0.72 (0.22)
Inpatient medical nights	0.23 (0.13)
Out-patient psychiatry attendances	0.39 (0.95)
Out-patient medical attendances	1.29 (2.08)
Accident and Emergency attendances	1.48 (1.76)
Community health services	
General practitioner consultations	3.55 (2.68)
Dentist contacts	1.25 (0.45)
Social services	
Field social worker contacts	14.41 (13.63)
Leaving care worker contacts	8.43 (25.52)
Family support worker contacts	1.10 (0.22)
Education services	
Education welfare officer contacts	7.43 (12.60)
School nurse contacts	0.65 (0.11)
Youth justice sector services	
Contact with the police	8.43 (21.28)
Youth custody contacts	1.11 (1.89)
Private sector services	
Optician contacts	1.61 (1.01)
Therapist contacts	28.0 (28.28)

Table 7.9 Total cost of all external services per resident over 12 months

	Mean (standard deviation) 2001/2002			
	All homes	Local authority provision	Non-statutory sector provision	p-value
Health services	690 (2,002)	208 (312)	1,470 (3,129)	.173
Social services	485 (705)	600 (859)	300 (274)	.233
Youth justice sector	119 (334)	80 (113)	181 (528)	.512
Education sector (excluding in-house education)	4,669 (5,310)	6,748 (5,625)	1,311 (2,246)	.000
Private sector	30 (125)	0 (0)	76 (198)	.192
Total cost of external services	5,993 (5,909)	7,637 (6,322)	3,338 (4,129)	.037
Total cost of homes (including in-house education)	82,341 (35,767)	79,609 (28,358)	86,754 (46,299)	.579
Total cost of packages of care	88,334 (35,487)	87,246 (29,593)	90,092 (44,700)	.824

UNIVARIATE ASSOCIATIONS WITH THE TOTAL COST OF CARE PACKAGES

Table 7.10 details the univariate relationships between the total cost of homes plus external services per resident per week and the pre-specified independent variables. At the 5 per cent level of statistical significance, higher costs were significantly associated with lower residents' well-being, a lower length of stay, a higher staff to resident ratio, a lower occupancy rate and being located in the south of England. Higher pressure to temptation prior to entry to the home was significant at the 10 per cent level of significance at least. Again, these relationships are in the expected direction.

Table 7.10 Univariate associations with the cost of homes plus external services per resident per week

Independent variable	Number of homes[1]	Mean cost (SD)	p-value
Age (mean)[2]			
≤ 14.57	19	1,549 (553)	
> 14.57	15	1,806 (787)	.113
Gender (% male)[2]			
≤ 60%	20	1,707 (615)	
> 60%	14	1,675 (789)	.900
Residents' well-being[2]			
Low well-being ≤ 57.5	19	1,923 (1,629)	
High well-being > 57.5	15	1,404 (434)	.032*
Staff satisfaction[2]			
Low staff satisfaction ≤ 42.8	14	1,807 (1,571)	
High staff satisfaction > 42.8	20	1,615 (1,253)	.1543
Staff perception of sufficiency of staff[2]			
Insufficient staff ≤ 8.67	18	1,741 (771)	
Sufficient staff > 8.67	36	1,642 (582)	.762
Delinquency prior to entry to home[3]			
No residents categorised as delinquent	6	1,283 (699)	
Some residents categorised as delinquent	26	1,723 (699)	.147
Pressure to temptation prior to entry to home[2]			
Low pressure ≤ 1.5	19	1,653 (765)	
High pressure > 1.5	15	1,746 (577)	.076*
Length of stay (mean)[2]			
≤ 311 days	19	2,050 (2,046)	
> 311 days	15	1,243 (240)	.009*

Continued on next page

Table 7.10 continued

Independent variable	Number of homes[1]	Mean cost (SD)	p-value
Staff to resident ratio[2]			
≤ 72.8%	18	1,525 (551)	
> 72.8%	16	1,884 (1,688)	.001*
Occupancy rate[2]			
≤ 85%	18	1,993 (1,998)	
> 85%	16	1,358 (390)	.000*
Waking night staff			
Yes	4	2,160 (424)	
No	29	1,598 (675)	.118
Sector			
Local authority	21	1,673 (568)	
Non-statutory	12	1,653 (850)	.937
In-house education provided			
Yes	12	1,575 (534)	
No	20	1,611 (577)	.859
Location			
South of England	8	2,366 (763)	
Other (Midlands or north of England)	25	1,442 (464)	.000*
Strategy relating to education and behaviour[2]			
Less positive strategies ≤ 7.60	16	2,033 (753)	
Positive strategies > 7.60	18	1,393 (441)	.147

Notes:
1 Some missing data.
2 Split at the median but analysed as continuous data.
3 As measured by young people's social workers.
*Statistically significant at the 10% level at least.

MULTIVARIATE ASSOCIATIONS WITH THE TOTAL COST OF CARE PACKAGES

The final multiple regression is shown in Table 7.11. The three independent variables found to be associated significantly with the total cost of homes plus external services per resident per week were pressure to temptation before entry to the home, the length of stay in the home and location of the home. On average, costs were higher the greater the pressure to temptation on young people before entry to the home, the shorter the length of stay in the home and for homes located in the south of England compared to elsewhere. The total cost of care packages in the south of England cost approximately £717 more per resident per week than elsewhere, on average. In terms of length of stay, there was a small reduction in cost per resident per week (less than £1) for every extra day spent in residential care, on average. The adjusted r^2 was 0.48, suggesting that the model was able to explain almost half of the variation in the total cost of care packages per resident, per week.

Table 7.11 Multiple regression for the cost of homes plus external services

Variables	£	95% confidence interval	p-value
Pressure to temptation before entry	106	7 to 205	.037
Length of stay	−0.88	−1.71 to 0.04	.040
South versus other	717	310 to 1123	.001

Findings from the generalised linear model with gamma distribution errors and the bootstrap regression analyses were similar to the simple linear regressions reported in the table, and so are not reported here. The final model from the home-based cost-function analysis was regressed on the cost of homes plus external services for completeness, but this was not found to enhance the model's efficiency.

General well-being

The young people's general well-being, based on self-report, is reported in Table 7.12. At entry to the study (T1), general well-being was statistically significantly higher for young people in non-statutory sector homes than those in local authority homes. Two analyses are presented for T2, the first including all those in the home at T1 who could be contacted at T2 (thus including some young people who had left the home since T1) and the second including only those young people who were resident in the home at both T1 and T2. Although the sample size for the latter group is smaller, this group includes those individuals most likely to have been influenced by the home in question and excludes those for whom outcomes may have been influenced by other factors, such as their location/placement since leaving the original home.

Both analyses show slightly higher scores for the non-statutory sector, but the differences are not statistically significant.

Table 7.12 Well-being of young people

	All homes		Local authority provision		Non-statutory provision		
	n	Mean (SD)	n	Mean (SD)	n	Mean (SD)	p-value
General well-being at T1	175	56.0 (27.5)	129	51.1 (27.8)	46	69.7 (21.3)	.000
General well-being at T2, including those who had left the home	113	61.8 (28.6)	77	61.7 (30.6)	24	64.5 (26.7)	.688
General well-being at T2, excluding those who had left the home	71	62.5 (31.0)	52	60.8 (32.8)	19	67.0 (25.6)	.459

SD = standard deviation

UNIVARIATE ASSOCIATIONS WITH GENERAL WELL-BEING

Table 7.13 details the univariate relationships between general well-being and the pre-specified independent variables. At the 5 per cent level of statistical significance, greater well-being was significantly associated with higher staff satisfaction, greater staff perception of the sufficiency of staff numbers, more positive managers' strategies relating to education and behaviour and being in the non-statutory sector, as compared to local authority provided homes.

MULTIVARIATE ASSOCIATIONS WITH WELL-BEING

After the process of backward elimination, the final multi-level model arrived at for general well-being is as follows, based on 141 young people. All coefficients that were kept in the model were statistically significant at the 5 per cent level.

Well-being=65.001 + .022 length of stay − 2.765 pressure to temptation before entering the home − 14.939 local authority

Table 7.13 Univariate associations with general well-being

Independent variable	Number of homes[1]	Mean cost (SD)	p-value
Age (mean)[2]			
≤ 14.33	21	59.4 (20.7)	
> 14.33	21	55.0 (16.1)	.469
Gender (% male)[2]			
≤ 60%	22	56.0 (17.7)	
> 60%	20	58.5 (19.6)	.535
Cost of home per resident per week[2]			
≤ £1,216	22	59.0 (16.9)	
> £1,216	20	55.3 (20.3)	.320
Staff satisfaction[2]			
Low staff satisfaction ≤ 42.6	22	53.7 (16.9)	
High staff satisfaction > 42.6	20	61.1 (19.7)	.044*
Staff perception of sufficiency of staff[2]			
Insufficient staff ≤ 8.67	21	50.5 (18.0)	
Sufficient staff > 8.67	21	63.9 (16.8)	.015*
Delinquency prior to entry to home[3]			
No residents categorised as delinquent	7	65.9 (21.3)	
Some residents categorised as delinquent	34	55.7 (17.5)	.183
Pressure to temptation prior to entry to home[2]			
Low pressure ≤ 1.85	21	60.5 (20.7)	
High pressure > 1.85	21	54.0 (15.7)	.439
Length of stay (mean)[2]			
≤ 308 days	19	50.9 (18.3)	
> 308 days	19	62.4 (16.9)	.114

Continued on next page

Table 7.13 continued

Independent variable	Number of homes[1]	Mean cost (SD)	p-value
Staff to resident ratio[2]			
≤ 71.5%	20	56.1 (17.1)	
> 71.5%	19	56.7 (19.6)	.873
Occupancy rate[2]			
≤ 83%	20	50.1 (18.3)	
> 83%	19	63.0 (15.8)	.115
Sector			
Local authority	30	51.9 (17.2)	
Non-statutory	12	70.1 (14.6)	.002*
Strategy relating to education and behaviour[2]			
Less positive strategies ≤ 7.00	17	55.4 (19.8)	
Positive strategies > 7.00	22	61.2 (17.1)	.034*

Notes:
1 Some missing data.
2 Split at the median but analysed as continuous data.
3 As measured by young people's social workers.
*Statistically significant at the 10% level at least.

On average, residents' well-being was found to be related significantly to length of stay and pressure to temptation before entering the home and sector. In terms of length of stay, which was positively related to well-being, the model predicts that for every additional day in the home, a young person will, on average, demonstrate an increase in well-being of .022 points on the well-being scale. Pressure to temptation before entry into the home was found to be related negatively to well-being such that the greater the pressure to temptation before entry, the worse the level of well-being within the home. In terms of sector, young people who resided in a local authority home were found to have poorer well-being than their non-statutory sector counterparts: reporting an average of 15 points lower. No significant associations were found between general well-being and either costs or managers' strategy relating to education and behaviour.

Further analysis of the data suggests that the managers' strategy relating to education and behaviour is a close substitute for sector of home. Removing sector and entering the strategy variable results in the following model:

Well-being=21.861 + .023 length of stay – 2.895 pressure to temptation before entering home + 4.459 strategy relating to education and behaviour

The log likelihood value for this model (an overall measure of model fit) was slightly worse than for the model with sector included but the difference is not significant at the 5 per cent level. This indicates that, although the model with sector included is marginally better in terms of model fit, there is little to choose between the two specifications. The implication of the two models is that the finding that sector is important in determining well-being can be explained largely through the role of the managers' strategy.

Cost-effectiveness

Exploration of cost-effectiveness is not easy given the design of the study. However, a tentative exploration of relative cost-effectiveness between homes provided by the local authority and non-statutory sectors revealed little difference in costs or effects. Local authority costs were found to be £1,491 as compared to £1,664 in the non-statutory sector, giving a difference of £173 per resident per week that was not statistically significant. Outcomes at T1 (the period with the most powerful data due to the larger number of responses) were 51.1 points on the ladder for young people in local authority homes compared to 69.7 for those in the non-statutory sector, a statistically significant difference of 18.6 points.

These results suggest that the non-statutory sector is able to produce significantly better outcomes for similar levels of expenditure. Outcomes at T2 (the period most comparable with the cost data) were 61.7 points on the ladder for young people in local authority homes compared to 64.5 for those in the non-statutory sector, a non-significant difference of only 2.8 points. The difference using the smaller sample of those in the home at both T1 and T2 was slightly larger (6.2 points) but remained a non-significant difference. Given these small and statistically insignificant differences in both costs and effects, it appears that similar outcomes were derived from similar levels of expenditure irrespective of sector. In order to take into consideration the significant differences in baseline well-being scores, T2 scores by sector were adjusted for T1 scores, but differences in T2 scores remained statistically non-significant. Nor were there any significant differences between the local authority and non-statutory sectors in terms of the change in outcome scores between T1 and T2.

Discussion

Cost of homes

The current study estimated the average cost of children's homes to be £1,543 per resident per week, ranging from £622 to £3,823. Previous studies have found similar results. A recent report by Berridge *et al.* (2002) estimated the costs of six children's homes to range between £1,240 and £2,037 per week, excluding one highly expensive single-child placement. Similarly, children's and families' residential care services for England were calculated to cost £1,929 per resident per week, on average (CIPFA 2002). Hughes (1988) also found substantial variation in costs of residential care for children between local authorities. For example, the cost of inner London homes was over 80 per cent of the cost of the least costly homes included in the sample.

Local authority residential care in the current sample was found to be lower in cost than non-statutory sector care, but this difference in cost was not statistically significant and was due mainly to the greater provision of in-house education in the non-statutory sector, a cost that is borne by the education authority where no in-house education is provided. This finding contrasts with the common perception that non-statutory sector providers are more expensive than local authority own provision.

The cost of homes was found to be associated significantly with the location of the home and staff to resident ratio, with homes in the south of England and those with a higher staff to resident ratio being relatively more expensive. These findings are not surprising given the much higher prices in the south of England and the significant contribution staff costs make to the total cost of children's homes (approximately 65% in the current sample). Thus the variation in the cost of homes can be explained more by home level characteristics than variation in the characteristics of young people or staff.

Cost of broader care packages

In order to get an idea of the broader costs involved in the care of young people in residential care, costs external to the home were estimated. The greatest burden outside the homes fell on the education sector. The total costs of care packages, including the cost of homes and the cost of external services, were found to be associated significantly with the location of the home (as in the cost of homes model), young people who had experienced pressure to temptation prior to entry to the home and the length of stay of the resident in the home. Higher costs were associated with young people who had experienced more pressure to temptation prior to entry to the home, being located in the south of England and shorter lengths of stay. The questionnaire response rate in terms of residents' use of external services was low and likely to contain inaccuracies, so these results must be treated with caution.

Outcomes

Economic analysis is concerned not just with costs but also with the outcomes generated by costs and the relationship between the two variables. Outcomes were explored using a measure of general well-being. In our first multi-level model, greater well-being was associated with longer lengths of resident stay, lower levels of pressure to temptation prior to entry to the home and being in the non-statutory sector. The first two results are intuitive. Longer lengths of resident stay suggest greater stability and perhaps a lower proportion of more chaotic and frequently moving young people. This result is supported by Friman *et al.* (1996), who also found a positive relationship between length of stay and well-being. Similarly, lower pressures to temptation prior to entry to home suggest either residents who are not particularly vulnerable to such pressure or residents who were previously in a more stable environment.

The lower well-being demonstrated by residents in local authority homes at T1 is more difficult to interpret. The main problem is determining the causality. Does being in a local authority home reduce well-being, on average, or does well-being tend to be lower in young people who enter local authority homes? It is possible, for example, that young people with poorer well-being were more likely to enter local authority homes. It is not possible to determine causation accurately because we do not have measures of well-being for young people before they entered the homes they were in at T1. To explore this further would require residents to be followed from the point of entry to a home over time, which was not possible in the current study. It is worth noting that this was virtually the only outcome variable that suggested that local authority sector residents were on average 'worse off' than those in the independent sector. In addition, well-being at T2 was more or less equal between the two groups, suggesting improvements in the well-being of residents in local authority homes over time.

Our second multi-level model additionally revealed a positive relationship between managers' strategy relating to education and behaviour and general well-being of the young people in the homes, such that greater well-being was associated with more positive strategies. This relationship was complex and further analysis of the data suggested that managers' strategy on education and behaviour was a close substitute for sector of home. This finding suggests that the independent sector obtained its 'better results' as a result of more positive management strategies.

It is also interesting to note that well-being was not found to be influenced significantly by the cost of homes in either univariate or multi-variate analysis; therefore, the resources available to homes do not appear to be a factor in the well-being of residents. The implication of this finding is uncertain, but perhaps the most likely is that other factors are simply more important. Lower well-being at study entry was found to be a predictor of higher total costs (cost of homes plus external services) over the subsequent months in univariate analysis, providing some evidence to suggest that resources are being targeted at those homes containing unhappier young people – in other words, those likely to be in more need.

Key variables

Length of stay within the home and pressure to temptation prior to entry to the home were found to be related significantly to both costs and outcomes in multiple regression. As length of stay increased, the total cost of care packages per resident per week fell and outcomes improved, suggesting that better outcomes can be achieved at lower cost if movement between placements is minimised. This may reflect a tendency among more difficult residents to move frequently. Alternatively, the stability implied by lack of movement may itself have a good effect. Conversely, as pressure to temptation prior to entry to the home increased, the total cost of care packages per resident per week increased and outcomes worsened. Thus, strategies to reduce movement between placements and pressures to temptation should be encouraged.

Also of interest is the finding that while the total cost of homes per resident per week increases as the staff to resident ratio rises, this does not seem to have an impact on the outcomes experienced by young people, suggesting that increasing the staff to resident ratio is not necessarily the most appropriate strategy for improving outcomes. That said, it is possible that those homes with higher staff to resident ratios were looking after the more difficult and complex young people: young people whose outcomes may well be poor relative to those in homes with lower staff to resident ratios.

Cost-effectiveness

Exploration of the relative cost-effectiveness of local authority versus independent sector provision revealed only small differences in costs and effects between the two sectors. Two analyses were undertaken, one suggesting that similar outcomes were achieved for similar levels of expenditure, and the other suggesting that the non-statutory sector was able to produce significantly better outcomes for similar levels of expenditure. The latter analysis was more methodologically sound, using T2 outcome data, but was limited statistically by lower sample sizes and potentially greater bias, so it is not possible to come to any firm conclusions.

Limitations

The data used in this economic analysis have their limitations. Of particular concern was the poor completion of the questionnaires reporting use of external services and thus these results must be treated with special caution. Further exploration of the cost-effectiveness of children's homes was not possible as a result of the lack of a control group. The cost-effectiveness analysis presented in this chapter was a tentative exploration of local authority versus non-statutory sector homes. While this analysis provides some useful insights, the possibility of bias between the two groups cannot be ruled out. As a result of the detail in our assessments and the practical and resource constraints within which we were operating, we had to concentrate on a relatively small number of homes (n=45), which, in terms of the statistical analysis, lowered the statistical power of the study and limited the types of analysis that it was possible to undertake and the confidence with which we can present our findings. At the individual level, sample sizes were much smaller at T2 than at T1 because of the difficulty of tracing individuals who had left the home. Nonetheless, this work represents the first significant attempt to explore the costs and outcomes of children's homes in the UK and, given the complexity and resource intensity of research carried out in institutional facilities, the sample sizes were in fact an important achievement.

Summary

- The total cost of children's homes (including in-house education costs where relevant) per resident per week was estimated to be around £1,500.

- Staff costs accounted for 65 per cent of the total cost of children's homes.

- Although non-statutory sector homes were estimated to be more expensive than local authority homes, this difference was not statistically significant and disappeared when in-house education, more often provided in the non-statutory sector, was removed.

- There was no statistically significant difference in the total cost of care packages (costs of residential care plus services external to the homes) per resident when comparing local authority and non-statutory sectors.

- Higher costs of homes were significantly associated with being located in the south of England and having a relatively high staff to resident ratio.

- Higher total costs of care packages (including costs of the services external to the homes) were significantly associated with pressure to temptation prior to entry to the home, shorter lengths of stay and, again, being located in the south of England.

- Outcomes were higher for those young people with longer lengths of stay in the home and for those who reported lower pressures to temptation before entry into the home.

- Outcomes for young people were lower in local authority homes compared to the non-statutory sector at T1, but equivalent at T2.

- Greater well-being for young people was associated with a more positive manager's strategy relating to education and behaviour.

- Increased lengths of stay in the homes were significantly associated with lower total costs of care packages per resident per week and better outcomes.

- Increased pressure to temptation prior to entry to the home was significantly associated with higher total costs of care packages per resident per week and poorer outcomes.

- Increased staff to resident ratios were associated with higher total costs of homes, but did not have a significant impact on outcomes.

- Total cost per resident per week was not found to be related to the well-being of young people in the home.

This part of the study has explored variations in cost across children's homes and differences in cost between local authority and non-statutory sector provision. Knowing the limitations of the study design, the analyses presented should be seen as exploratory and hypothesis generating, rather than explanatory. A number of the findings, however, were logical and intuitive, thus strengthening the confidence we can have in the results. In particular, the significant impact of a southerly location or a relatively large staff to resident ratio on costs, and the significant impact of length of stay and pressure to temptation on well-being, are intuitive findings.

Tentative exploration of relative cost-effectiveness was inconclusive but suggested that there was little difference in the cost-effectiveness of local authority versus non-statutory sector provided homes. Our results also provided evidence to suggest that managers exercising a more positive strategy relating to education and behaviour had a more positive impact on well-being. We move on now to Chapter 8, where this point will be explored further and where we employ a different technique to look at a wider range of outcomes for young people.

What Makes a Difference to Outcomes for Young People?

Introduction

As we have seen, children's homes vary. Their residents differ in their characteristics. They are led in different ways. Their costs vary considerably. However, are these differences associated with differences in outcomes for young people? If so, are the differences explicable purely in terms of the characteristics of the residents or do the kind of leadership, for example, and the resources available also play a part? This chapter considers these questions.

Method

Our primary method of analysis, multi-level modelling, takes account of the context in which young people live. As we noted in Chapter 7, the method is suitable for use in most situations where individuals are 'nested' within units that may in turn be nested within others. This, of course, is the case with our research.

The outcomes in which we were interested were of varying kinds. In this chapter we examine:

- the behaviour of young people while living in the children's home (offending, running away, school exclusion)
- the well-being of young people while living in the home and afterwards
- young people's perceptions of the social climate of the home

- psycho-social functioning of the young people while living in the home and afterwards
- staff morale
- staff perceptions of the functioning of the home.

Our aim was to see how far our ratings of leadership characteristics added to our ability to explain outcomes after allowing for resident characteristics. In general we sought to develop explanations for the outcomes in four steps.[1]

First, we tried to obtain the 'best' prediction we could of these outcomes based on variables at the individual level. Which set of 'individual variables' we used depended on the outcome we were trying to explain. For example, one outcome was 'reconviction in the home'. In seeking to explain this, we used four variables: age, sex, whether previously convicted or cautioned and whether previously suspended from school. We used these variables for practical reasons – they were available in the same data set – and for logical ones – we expected the two to be connected. We also used length of time in the home because the longer a young person was resident the more chance she or he had to commit an offence.

By going for the 'best' combination of individual variables we were inevitably 'overfitting' our model at level 1. Chance variations should mean that it explained more than it would if repeated. This, however, mattered less than it might. We were using the individual variables not because we were particularly interested in them but in order to ensure that associations that we found at level 2 were not explained by a failure to take account of the intake of homes.

Our second step was to add in the level 2 variables. Our key interest was in leadership characteristics and, as described later, we developed four measures of these. In each model we added these four variables to the best selection of variables at level 1. We then successively dropped the level 2 variables that were not significantly associated with outcome until either all were dropped or some remained. Then we retested the ones we had dropped individually to ensure that they were not significant at this point. In practice, the four variables proved to have quite high correlations among themselves. This made interpretation of the results difficult. So we also followed a practice of 'forward estimation'. In this we entered each of the four variables individually and then examined the effects of adding the others to them. These procedures yielded us our main level 2 model.

Our third step was to examine whether the sector of the homes and their costs related to outcomes.

This led us to our fourth step in which we tried to explain which causal processes might be involved.

Before undertaking our main analysis, we needed to do some preliminary work on the leadership ratings that were our key independent variables.

Leadership ratings

We had nine ratings, many of which were strongly related to each other.[2] Inspection suggested that eight of the ratings fell into three distinct clusters, which left a single rating as a 'stand alone'.

We called the first group of three ratings the 'management cluster'. The ratings related respectively to whether the manager of the home had a permanent post or was 'acting up', the clarity of the manager's role and the time the manager spent in the unit. Table 8.1 gives the correlations between these variables. As can be seen, recognised seniority goes with greater clarity of role and less time in the unit. We created a variable 'manager' by adding the ratings for 'status of post' and 'role clarity' and subtracting the rating for 'time spent in unit'.

Table 8.1 Correlation coefficients for 'management' items

		Status of post	Clarity in own role	Time spent in unit
Status of post	Pearson correlation			
	Sig. (2-tailed)	–	–	–
	N			
Clarity in own role	Pearson correlation	.443**		
	Sig. (2-tailed)	.004	–	–
	N	40		
Time spent in unit	Pearson correlation	–.326*	–.479**	
	Sig. (2-tailed)	.040	.002	–
	N	40	40	

Notes:
*Correlation is significant at the .05 level (2-tailed test).
**Correlation is significant at the .01 level (2-tailed test).

The second cluster, again consisting of three ratings, we called 'influence'. The ratings were related to the manager's 'experience with team', 'autonomy' and 'influence on practice'. Managers who were high on influence would convey the impression that they had freedom of action, a team which they felt was their own and a considerable influence on practice. Table 8.2 shows that these three ratings went together and we created a score by adding them.

Table 8.2 Correlation coefficients for 'influence' items

		Experience with team	Autonomy	Influence on practice
Experience with team	Pearson correlation			
	Sig. (2-tailed)	–	–	–
	N			
Autonomy	Pearson correlation	.545**		
	Sig. (2-tailed)	.000	–	–
	N	40		
Influence on practice	Pearson correlation	.693**	.619**	
	Sig. (2-tailed)	.000	.000	–
	N	40	40	

Note: **Correlation is significant at the .01 level (2-tailed test).

Our third cluster consisted of two ratings. These related to the quality of the manager's strategy for 'behaviour' and strategy for managing 'education', as we assessed them. Again the two ratings were highly correlated ($r=.715$; $p<.001$) and we created a score by adding them.

There remained one rating, 'external support', which we did not assign to a cluster. It was in fact negatively associated with ratings in the 'influence' cluster. Managers who had high ratings on 'external support' typically had low ones for 'autonomy', 'experience with team' and 'influence on practice'. Nevertheless, it seemed to be conceptually distinct from this 'influence' cluster and we left it as a single rating.

We called these combined variables 'external support', 'strategy', 'manager', and 'key role' (i.e. influential). Our final correlation matrix shows that even with this degree of simplification, (Table 8.3) correlations among these variables was still quite high.

How far did these leadership ratings explain our measures of outcomes for young people?

Table 8.3 Correlation coefficients for combined variables

		External support	Strategy	Manager	Keyrole
External support	Pearson correlation				
	Sig. (2-tailed)	–	–	–	–
	N				
Strategy	Pearson correlation	–.246			
	Sig. (2-tailed)	.126	–	–	–
	N	40			
Manager	Pearson correlation	.167	.496**		
	Sig. (2-tailed)	.126	.001	–	–
	N	40	40		
Keyrole	Pearson correlation	.167	.488**	.308	
	Sig. (2-tailed)	.303	.001	.054	–
	N	40	40	40	

Note: **Correlation is significant at the 0.01 level (2-tailed).

Behaviour

We began by using our questionnaire known as the T1 *Resident Log.* This provided basic but useful information on all the young people who had been resident in the home at any time in the previous year as well as those who were still there. It also told us whether a young person had been convicted or cautioned for an offence, had run away, or had been excluded from school at any time while living in the home. These were the outcomes which we wished to predict.

In seeking to predict them, we used information on the young people's age, sex, ethnicity (ethnic minority or other), length of stay in the home (period at risk), previous convictions or cautions, and whether they had been excluded previously from school. Children under the age of ten were excluded from this analysis.

Behaviour: conviction

Our analysis showed that the key individual variables in predicting reconviction were length of time in the home (period at risk) and whether the young person previously had been excluded from school. After allowing for these factors, our combined variable 'strategy' was strongly related to outcome (p<.005). Thus those managers who, from our perspective, had clear, well-worked out strategies for dealing with behavioural problems and working appropriately in respect of education had better results.

Our variable 'manager' was also significantly related to outcome and the relationships with 'keyrole' (our measure of influence) and 'external support' were in the predicted direction. Thus managers of homes who in our judgement had a clear role and were confirmed in post also had better results. However, the association only held because they also tended to have good strategies.[3] Status and clarity of role may help in establishing good strategies. They do not in themselves replace the need for a sensible approach to managing behavioural difficulties.

As a check on our model, we tested it in relation to young people about whom we had information at T2 and whose length of stay in the home was such that they should not have been resident at T1. 'Strategy' was again associated with outcome at a high level of significance. So too were 'manager' and 'keyrole' when these were introduced into the analysis on their own.

The most likely explanation for these findings was that the best 'recipe' for keeping the level of delinquency low lies in clear, well-worked out strategies, delivered by managers with high status and clear roles, and which are owned by staff teams. As there is a strong degree of correlation between all these variables, it is difficult, and may well be misleading, to allocate particular degrees of influence to any one factor on its own.

Behaviour: running away

The analysis of 'running away' is reported quickly. A number of individual variables – length of stay, age, previous convictions and whether previously excluded from school – were related to this outcome. None of our leadership ratings was significantly related to it.

Behaviour: exclusion from school

The results for school exclusion were very similar to those for conviction. 'Strategy' was very strongly related to low school exclusion rates (p<.001) after we had allowed for individual variables related to exclusion (age, previous convictions and length of time in the home).

'Management role' and 'influence' were also related to this outcome if put into the analysis on their own. If put in together with 'strategy', their effects were swamped.

This model was validated on our T2 data. Again 'strategy' predicted good outcomes on this variable, as did 'management role' if put in on its own. 'Influence' was related to outcomes in the predicted direction but the association was no longer significant. Once again, 'management role' ceased to have a significant relationship with outcome if put in together with 'strategy'.

Unsocial behaviour

We created a variable 'unsocial behaviour'. This ran from 0 to 3. Those who scored 3 had run away from the home, been cautioned or convicted for an offence committed while resident, and been excluded from school while living there. Those who scored 0 had done none of those things. Those who scored 1 or 2 had done one or two of them respectively.

This outcome was most efficiently predicted by age, previous convictions, length of stay and our strategy variable. Those least likely to behave in an 'unsocial way' were those who had spent a brief time in the home, had no previous convictions, were relatively young, and were living in homes where the manager had clear well-worked out strategies for managing 'education' and 'behavioural difficulties'.

Well-being of young people

We had four measures of well-being. These were:

1. 'Ladder' – young people marked their happiness on a ladder. A mark near the top of the ladder meant high well-being, one near the bottom low well-being (see details in Chapter 7).

2. 'Happiness' – a four-point rating of 'How happy would you say your life has been overall?'

3. 'Feeling' – a seven-point rating of 'How do you feel about your life overall?'

4. 'Esteem'– a measure created from the answers by the young people to questions about how they were feeling and how they felt their lives were going.

We measured these on the basis of the *Questionnaire to Young People* at T1. We also examined the effect of the home on changes over time. To do this, we used data about the 72 young people for whom we had scores at both points in time. Our analysis yielded little explanation in terms of 'happiness', 'feeling' and 'esteem', but confirmed the conclusion drawn in Chapter 7 in respect of the 'ladder'.

The young people's well-being on this ladder variable was predicted by a combination of four variables: length of stay, a measure of 'pressure to temptation' on the young person before entry to the home, strategy and influence. Young people were less likely to feel happy if 1. they were relatively recent arrivals, 2. they had, as we measured it, been under a relatively high degree of pressure before entry, and 3. they were living in homes where the manager did not have clear, well-worked out strategies.

Residents' perceptions of social climate

As already described, we measured four aspects of the residents' perceptions of the home. These were:

1. how far the home was seen as a friendly place
2. how far the home was seen as a well-behaved place
3. how far the residents seemed to be involved in the running of the home
4. how far resident morale seemed to be high.

We formed a summary measure of 'social climate' by adding the variables listed earlier. In addition, we had a measure of how far the residents were happy with certain aspects of the home.

The main individual variable which predicted these perceptions was our measure of 'pressure before entry to the home'. After we had taken this into account, the main leadership rating that predicted these outcomes was 'strategy'. This significantly predicted good outcomes for 'home friendliness' and 'behaviour', and also our overall measure of 'social climate'. Its relationships with 'resident morale' and 'involvement' were not significant, although they were in the predicted direction.

An unpredicted finding was that high 'external support' was negatively related to the 'involvement of residents' in the running of the home. Again this could be a chance finding, reflecting the involvement of external management when a home is in difficulty or, conceivably, reflecting the difficulty of responding both to a supportive external management and to the young people. There was a similar negative result for 'influence' that was negatively associated with 'behaviour' after strategy had been taken into account.

Psycho-social development of the residents

We measured the psycho-social well-being of the residents through an instrument based on the 'Looking After Children' (LAC) dimensions (Parker et al. 1991). Each resident was given a score based on her or his behaviour, performance at school, close ties with at least one adult and so on (for details, please see Appendix B, 'Sample Models').

The best predictor was based on a measure of prior family support (see Appendix B) as rated by the social workers and the strategy score. Children had better functioning if they were said to have come from relatively supportive homes and were living in children's homes where the manager had a clear well-worked out strategy for managing behaviour and educational issues.

Where the young people remained in the same home, they continued to do 'better' if the manager had clear strategies, although the numbers were too small for the association to be significant. Where they had gone elsewhere, there was a small non-significant association between their well-being score and the strategy variable.

The most likely explanation for this result is that the home had a temporary effect on the well-being of its residents but that this was eroded when they left. There is evidence elsewhere for this kind of effect (Allerhand et al. 1966; Sinclair 1971). In keeping with this interpretation, there was a negative relationship between *change* on the well-being score and the presence of good strategies. Where the young people remained in the home, the association was neither marked nor significant. Where they had moved elsewhere, the association was stronger and significant at the .05 level.

Staff perceptions of social climate of the home

We looked at the same four main variables from the staff perspective. Essentially we asked them to say whether the young people:

1. perceived the home as friendly
2. saw it as well behaved
3. felt that they were involved in its running
4. felt that morale in the home was high.

In summary:

- Staff working in homes with clear well-worked out strategies felt that the home was better behaved (management also had a good effect on this variable but the effect was lost if strategy was entered at the same time).

- The leadership variables were unrelated to how friendly the home was seen as being, the perceived morale of its residents, or its perceived friendliness.

Staff perceptions of guidance

We measured how far staff felt that they had been:

- well inducted into the job
- given clear guidance on how to deal with the young people
- given clear general guidance on what else was expected of them.

Individual variables that predicted these variables differed. Staff who had been a long time in post were less likely to feel that they had been well inducted. Staff who worked full-time were more likely to feel that they had good general guidance. After allowing for these differences, we found that:

- strategy was significantly and positively related to all three variables
- management was significantly and positively related to general guidance
- neither 'influence' nor 'external support' was significantly related to any of the three variables.

We also looked at measures of staff satisfaction and their overall concerns:

- Concerns were lower if the member of staff was 1. male, and 2. older. After allowing for this, the only leadership variable associated with low concerns was strategy.
- Job satisfaction was predicted by age and strategy (management was also significantly associated with job satisfaction but not if age was taken into account).
- Satisfaction with leadership was strongly associated with strategy but not with any other individual variable or with the other three measures of leadership.
- Satisfaction with the staffing ratio was positively associated with strategy but not with any of the other variables we investigated, including costs.
- Satisfaction with training was positively associated with age and strategy but not with other leadership variables.
- Neither our individual nor our leadership variables predicted staff cohesion.

Effect of costs

Chapter 7 explored the relationship between costs and well-being, as measured by the ladder in the general well-being section of the *Lancashire Quality of Life Profile* (Oliver *et al.* 1997). In this section, we look at the effect of costs on other outcomes.

The apparent effects on behaviour were relatively clear-cut:

- Higher costs were associated with a greater likelihood of young people being convicted or cautioned, but the relationship only became statistically significant if allowance was made for sector. Within sectors, more expensive homes were more likely to have higher conviction rates. Causality is difficult to determine. This finding may suggest that resources are higher in homes with more difficult young people and that we failed to take sufficient account of intake in our model. Alternatively, costs may rise with trouble – because, for example, the effective staffing ratio increases as children leave because of conviction or the management tries to increase control by restricting intake.

- The higher the cost the less likely the young person was to be excluded from school while living in the home. This finding is likely to result from the provision of on-site education by some homes, which will increase the cost of those homes but at the same time increase the likelihood of residents being included in school. The effect was not apparent if costs were calculated without including education.

- This effect also dropped below significance if sector was included. Young people living in homes in the non-statutory sector were less likely to be excluded from school in all models. This is likely to reflect the fact that a greater proportion of homes in the non-statutory sector provided on-site education than was the case for local authority homes.

There were rather similar results in relation to the young people's perceptions of the home:

- After allowing for individual variables, higher costs were associated with more negative perceptions of the home's friendliness, involvement of residents and morale. Again acknowledging concerns regarding causality, this suggestion that 'unhappier' homes are more expensive is perhaps a result of proactive targeting of resources to such homes, but may simply reflect the fact that 'unhappy' young people are likely to be more expensive in terms of service requirements, staff input and the like.

In terms of the happiness of the young people, the results were less clear-cut. All the associations between cost and our four measures of 'happiness' were negative, but this effect was only significant in one case and when sector was included in the equation. The suggestion of a negative relationship may, again, be due to the targeting of resources to 'unhappier' homes (e.g. by increasing the staff ratio in order to maintain order) or to the possibility that 'unhappier' young people are inherently more expensive to care for.

Costs were not found to be associated with our measure of psycho-social well-being or any of our outcome measures in the *Staff Questionnaire*. On these measures, expensive homes did neither better nor worse.

Effect of sector

In this section, we examine whether the location of the home in the non-statutory or local authority sector made a difference:

- In terms of behaviour, young people were less likely to be convicted or cautioned if the homes were in the non-statutory sector. This remained true if we allowed for costs and strategy.

- Young people in the non-statutory sector saw their homes as 'better behaved' but not as friendlier, more participatory or as having higher morale.

- Young people in the non-statutory sector assessed themselves as happier in terms of general well-being (as measured by the ladder).

Sector was not found to be associated with our measure of psycho-social well-being, but marked sector differences were found on the outcome measures contained in the *Staff Questionnaire*. In brief, staff in the non-statutory sector:

- were more satisfied with their jobs, their training, the leadership in the home (a variable that did not quite reach significance) and the number of staff in the home

- perceived the home as being friendlier and as having a much better standard of behaviour

- were more satisfied with the general guidance they were given, the guidance they had on dealing with the young people and their induction into the job.

The non-statutory sector and strategy

How far do the various associations we have been discussing reflect cause and effect? Three points should be made at the outset.

First, as can be seen from Appendix B, some of our models explain a relatively small amount of the variance. For example, homes vary considerably in our measure of resident morale. We explain none of this home variance through our home level variables. Some of this unexplained variance will no doubt arise from the 'turbulence' of homes. Children's homes are places where one thing leads to another. Thus a small change may lead to large unexpected falls in morale. Such effects are essentially unpredictable. Other parts of the variance may be unexplained because we selected inappropriate variables for our attempted explanation or did not measure them accurately.

Second, it does seem that there are processes that could be controlled, and which do lead to more or less good outcomes. The reason for thinking this is that the homes located in the non-statutory sector seemed to 'do better' on a number of outcomes and this was despite the fact that they appeared to take more 'problematic' residents. This does not mean that it was the fact of being non-statutory that made the difference. We did not take a random sample of homes from this sector. Those who volunteered may have been the more confident. Moreover, they differed from local authority homes in other ways – for example, because they were typically further from the residents' homes, a fact which enabled them to specialise and also may have insulated them from the effects of local delinquent cultures. Whatever the reason, it seems that the direction of cause and effect must flow from 'being in the non-statutory sector' to good outcomes rather than vice versa. This in turn raises the question of how the non-statutory sector produces these outcomes.

Third, a plausible candidate for the 'key ingredient' is our strategy variable. Homes where the manager received a 'good' strategy rating tended to have the following characteristics:

- lower reconviction/cautioning rates while residents in the home
- less exclusion from school while in the home
- more positive perceptions of the home social climate by residents
- more positive perceptions of the home social climate by staff
- higher well-being scores while residents were in the home
- happier residents (on some measures)
- more positive staff perceptions of the leadership and guidance in the home.

The ratings were made without any knowledge of the outcomes we have measured, which depended on the behaviour and views of residents and the views of staff. The associations do not therefore arise because those carrying out the ratings were influenced by the results. Nevertheless, there is a question as to whether strategy is the means whereby homes deliver results, or whether it is just associated with something else that does, or even simply a measure of the confidence of managers of homes with good results.

Our evidence on this suggests, but does not finally prove, that strategy is key. There are two reasons for thinking this:

1. Where strategy is entered along with 'being in non-statutory sector', one or other tends to mask the effect of the other (for example, neither variable has a significant association with staff satisfaction with induction although both are significantly associated with this on their own). This pattern suggests that the non-statutory sector achieves its outcomes through strategy or something closely associated with it.

2. A number of variables – proportion of permanent staff, management role of head of home, influence of manager on team, whether home had change of manager or function during the research – are strongly associated with strategy but are either negatively or non-significantly associated with outcomes when entered with strategy. This suggests that these variables make it easier for the manager to develop an effective strategy. If, however, she or he does not produce a good strategy given these favourable conditions, the results are no better than if the conditions did not apply.

So overall the most plausible explanation of these findings is to us as follows:

- Certain variables – stability, the clear management position of the manager of home, a high proportion of permanent staff, the degree to which a manager is at ease with and leads her or his team – make it much easier for a manager to put a good strategy in place. If, however, she or he does not put a good strategy in place, these variables do not have an impact on outcome.

- Other variables can be seen in a sense as 'part of strategy'. These may include good induction systems, the communication of clear messages to staff and the presence of a good keyworker system.

- There is no evidence that high expenditure is effective in producing good results. In some models it has a negative association with outcome. What matters is good practice and this is not ensured by either high staff numbers or high expenditure.

Summary

The ratings discussed in this chapter were based on interviews with managers of homes. As noted previously, the interview ratings were completed without awareness of the views of the staff and young people or knowledge of the findings on the young people's behaviour. Despite this limitation, the ratings proved able to predict many aspects of the behaviour of the young people, their well-being and the views of the staff.

One variable, 'strategy', dominated most. In homes where the manager had, in our opinion, clear well-worked out strategies for dealing with behaviour and education, staff had higher morale, felt that they received clearer and better guidance, and perceived that the young people behaved better. Young people were less likely to be excluded from school and less likely to be convicted or cautioned while in the home. They also expressed more favourable views about the social climate of the home, were happier on some measures, and were seen as functioning better by their field social workers. In theory, these apparently good effects could be explained by an easier intake. However, our analysis took account of background variables in so far as it could. Moreover, the temporary nature of at least one 'improvement' suggested that this was indeed brought about by the home.

Strategies were, it seemed, more likely to exist where the manager had a clear sanctioned management role and where she or he was influential – having a relatively high degree of autonomy and seeing themselves as the leader of a team whose practice they influenced. These aspects of leadership were, however, generally not enough on their own. Managers not only had to have position and influence; they also had to have clear strategies for the practice they wanted and an ability to ensure that this was enshrined in guidance, induction and so on.

Given the importance of practice, it was not surprising that costs seemed, on the whole, to have little or, if anything, a negative impact on outcomes. In this, it contrasted with the influence of sector.

This chapter reaffirms and develops the finding from Chapter 7 that greater well-being for young people was associated with having clear, operable strategies for ensuring they receive education and improving their behaviour. By means of a different technique, the chapter shows that this applies to a wider range of outcomes. It also supports the findings of the qualitative analysis by demonstrating that effective strategies have to be built by means of management structures ('management') and leadership of the staff team ('influence').

Overall, the large variations in cost that exist between non-specialist children's homes probably make little difference to outcomes. What seems to matter is that the manager is accepted as embodying good practice from within a clear ethos, has positive strategies for working both with the behaviour of young people and in relation to their education, and is capable of enabling staff to reflect and deploy these.

The next and final chapter will examine the implications of the findings from our research overall.

Notes

1   As will be seen, the method we followed was basically the same as that followed in the main economic section of the report. Our aim, however, was to test hypotheses about leadership style and for this reason we followed a slightly different method seeking to explain as much as possible at the individual level before introducing our level 2 variables. The wider set of outcomes considered also required us to use different data bases and different sets of variables in our analyses. As described, we also used some 'forward estimation'.

2   As an illustration of this point, we created a score by adding the ratings together. Seven of the ratings were positively correlated with this total (status of post .44, experience with team .79, autonomy .50, manager's influence on practice .66, quality of manager's strategy for managing behaviour .71, quality of manager's strategy for education .72). By contrast, the correlation with time in unit was −.22, and for external support −.03.

3   That is, if the two variables 'strategy' and 'keyrole' were put into the analysis together, only strategy emerged as significantly associated with outcome.

Chapter 9

Conclusions and Implications

Introduction

Effectively managing and staffing children's homes in England and Wales has provided challenges over recent decades, many of which have arisen from or resulted in crisis and scandal. The net effect of these has prompted an intensity of initiatives which have improvement at their heart. Some of these have addressed residential child care directly (e.g. Department of Health 2002; TOPSS 2003). More recently, this commitment has encompassed proposals for the registration of residential social care workers (General Social Care Council 2006).

Other initiatives, as observed in the introduction to Chapter 1, have been geared towards the overall enhancement of public care for children. The wide ranging government Green Paper *Care Matters: Transforming the Lives of Children and Young People in Care* (Department for Education and Skills 2006a) indicates the most recent government aspirations with regard to transforming the quality of the looked after system. The well-being of children and young people, and in particular of those who are in public care, is central to contemporary awareness at the levels of both policy and practice.

The problems associated with inconsistencies and variation in what residential child care is seen to achieve are long-standing in their nature. Our research set out to illuminate these and to go some way towards resolving them. The combination of methods we used was unusually complex, drawing extensively on statistical analyses, detailed qualitative approaches and economics. These were linked together by the systematic use of multi-level modelling. In these respects our research was ambitious. While research does not occupy a position to effect the transformation of problems, from our analyses we find that we are able to point towards areas of practice, policy and priorities that we feel may be strengthened or adjusted in order to reduce the likelihood of longer-term negative experiences for young people. That is our central aim in the present chapter.

In order to retain close links between findings and the suggestions we make, in this final chapter we highlight the key messages from the project overall. We hope that this level of repetition assists by staying close to the logical progression of the project and the way we have presented it through-out – that is, by building on description and analysis concerned with struc-ture, processes, resources and outcomes. After summarising detailed points raised by each methodological strand of the project, we discuss the main areas of importance in the direct management of children's homes. We then address the implications of these for practice and its management, chiefly in terms of policy and training.

Structure: the survey strand of the research

A key feature of this project lies in the diversity of the homes studied; the extensive survey data enabled us to depict their main characteristics and their variations. There were differences between children's homes in the sample in terms of:

- basic characteristics (e.g. size)
- the experience and characteristics of the staff
- age, sex and social history of the residents
- the length of time for which the residents stay
- the way the residents perceive the home
- staffing ratios
- staff/care hours
- whether staff thought there were sufficient numbers
- 'stressors' and sickness rates
- views on 'leadership'
- general staff morale.

We identified a number of concerns which arose from these differences. These mainly related to the young people living in children's homes, the staff working in the homes and the style of buildings used to provide residential care. Whether or not young people with complex and socially unacceptable behaviour may negatively influence other residents, and how to work with the behaviour of young people, were important issues. Differences in managers' approaches and the extent to which these resulted in differences in cost and outcomes were also a concern. There was considerable variation in staffing ratios and homes employed a mix of senior, and mostly trained, staff and younger, much less trained, staff; there was also a high turnover of staff. This implied that managers would not be able to rely on an ethos produced by pre-existing training for their younger staff. There were also major differences in the style of buildings used to provide residential care and little was known about the relationship of this to costs and outcomes.

The central concern emerging from this chapter was whether or not the variations identified would be apparent in outcomes for the young people, after allowing for differences in the young people prior to residence in the home.

Process: the qualitative strand of the research

On the basis of extensive accounts, we were able to provide a conceptualisation of what managers need to do to perform their tasks well. In practice, there was considerable variation between homes in the way they were managed. The research distinguished between these in terms of the ways they came to bear on the performance of the home. Nine key categorisations were identified and developed; these were:

External characteristics

1. status of post
2. clarity in own role/purpose and function
3. time able to spend within the unit
4. autonomy
5. external support.

Internal characteristics

6. experience with team
7. embodies high influence on practice
8. effective strategy for behaviour
9. effective strategy for education.

We showed that successful execution of the task is dependent upon factors that sit in dynamic relationship with each other, but are drawn from different contexts. In this way, we highlighted the importance of the influence which the manager exerts in terms of the internal and external contexts in which they operate. Interdependent arenas included individual managers' approaches within the home, with the staff group and with the group of young people, together with approaches in contextual arenas such as the organisation, other agencies, and the wider realm of policy and procedures. The effectiveness of managers relied on them being sufficiently well placed within each of these arenas to bring about consistent and reflective practice for and on behalf of the young people living in the care of the home itself. We showed that the accumulation of strengths in different arenas acts as an overall enabler of good practice.

Our conceptualisation of leadership took account of three main components: the developmental nature of the manager's role; the inter-relationship between what occurs in the home itself and what occurs in the external context; and the way the role is exercised. Of primary importance was achieving a collaborative team dynamic that worked consistently over time, and within the manager's preferred approach to practice.

Resources: the economics strand of the research

This part of the study explored variations in cost across children's homes and differences in cost between local authority and non-statutory sector provision. The analyses presented were seen as exploratory and hypothesis generating, rather than explanatory. A number of the findings, however, were logical and intuitive, thus strengthening the confidence we had in the results. In particular, the significant impact of a southerly location or a relatively large staff to resident ratio on costs, and the significant impact of length of stay and pressure to temptation on well-being, were intuitive findings. Tentative exploration of relative cost-effectiveness was inconclusive but suggested that there was little difference in the cost-effectiveness of local authority versus non-statutory sector provided homes. Our results also provided evidence to suggest that managers exercising a more positive strategy relating to education and behaviour had a more positive impact on well-being.

To summarise the main results from this section:

- The total cost of children's homes (including in-house education costs where relevant) per resident per week was estimated to be around £1,500.

- Staff costs accounted for 65 per cent of the total cost of children's homes.

- Although non-statutory sector homes were estimated to be more expensive than local authority homes, this difference was not statistically significant and disappeared when in-house education, more often provided in the non-statutory sector, was removed.

- There was no statistically significant difference in the total cost of care packages (costs of residential care plus services external to the homes) per resident when comparing local authority and non-statutory sectors.

- Higher costs of homes were significantly associated with being located in the south of England and having a relatively high staff to resident ratio.

- Higher total costs of care packages (including costs of the services external to the homes) were significantly associated with 'pressure to temptation' prior to entry to the home, shorter lengths of stay and, again, being located in the south of England.

- Outcomes were higher for those young people with longer lengths of stay in the home and for those who reported lower 'pressures to temptation' before entry into the home.

- Outcomes for young people were lower in local authority homes as compared to the non-statutory sector at T1 data collection, but equivalent at T2.

- Greater well-being for young people was associated with a more positive manager's strategy relating to education and behaviour.

- Increased lengths of stay in the homes were significantly associated with lower total costs of care packages per resident per week and better outcomes.

- Increased 'pressure to temptation' prior to entry to the home was significantly associated with higher total costs of care packages per resident per week and poorer outcomes.

- Increased staff to resident ratios were associated with higher total costs of homes, but did not have a significant impact on outcomes.

- Total cost per resident per week was not found to be related to the well-being of young people in the home.

Outcomes: from the multi-level modelling strand of the research

Our research investigated the influence of resources, differences between homes in terms of their intake and staffing, and leadership characteristics on outcomes for young people. The primary purpose of the multi-level analysis was to examine the relationship of the differences between homes and leadership characteristics to explaining outcomes for young people. The analysis included costs and a wide range of outcome measurements.

Our aim was to see how far our ratings of leadership characteristics, derived from the qualitative data, added to our ability to explain outcomes after allowing for resident characteristics. The interviews and ratings were carried out without awareness of the findings about the views of staff or young people or knowledge of the findings about the behaviour of and outcomes for the young people. Despite this, the ratings proved able to predict many aspects of how the children behaved, their well-being and the views of the staff. Costs, and a wider range of measurements of outcomes, were included in this part of our analysis.

One variable, 'strategy', dominated most. In homes where the manager had, in our assessment, clear well-worked out strategies for dealing with behaviour and education, staff had higher morale, felt that they received clearer and better guidance, and considered that the children behaved better. Young people were less likely to be excluded from school or to be convicted or cautioned while in the home. They also expressed more favourable views about the social climate of the home, were happier on some measures, and were seen as functioning better by their social workers. In theory, these apparently good effects could be explained by an easier intake. However, our analysis took account of background variables in so far as it could. Moreover, the temporary nature of at least one 'improvement' suggested that this was indeed brought about by the home.

Strategies were, it seemed, more likely to exist where managers had a clearly sanctioned management role and where they were influential – having a relatively high degree of autonomy and seeing themselves as the leader of a team whose practice they influenced. These aspects of leadership were, however, generally not enough on their own. Managers not only had to have position and influence; they also had to have clear strategies for the practice they wanted within the home and an ability to ensure this was enshrined in guidance, induction and so on.

Given the importance of practice, it was not surprising that the large variations in costs that exist between non-specialist children's homes appeared to make little difference to outcomes.

Overall, what seemed to matter in children's homes was that the manager:

- was accepted as embodying good practice from within a clear ethos

- had positive strategies for working both with the behaviour of young people and in relation to their education, and was capable of enabling staff to reflect and deploy these.

Main areas of importance in the direct management of children's homes

We have focused on developing an understanding of the major issues of the quality of residential environments, resources and the longer-term effectiveness of residential child care provision. The extensive survey data enabled us to depict main characteristics and their variation throughout the sample; the qualitative data provided a detailed picture of variations in the ways homes operate and are managed and led; and the economics data showed variations in the ways that resources are used, together with how much these cost. Thus, we have shown that children's homes are very varied places in terms of those who live and work in them, in the way that they are managed and led, and in the ways in which resources are used and their attendant costs.

Our analyses have led us to identify clearly the following issues:

- There are major differences in the ways homes function and, importantly, outcomes for young people are not determined by the numbers of staff involved, or by the costs of homes. A high level of expenditure and comparatively large numbers of staff may be necessary due to other considerations. However, such additional expenditure does not appear to promote the outcomes we measured.

- The influence that the *process* of providing care has on the kind of outcomes experienced by young people is of paramount importance – what managers and their staff do determines much of what is achieved for and on behalf of young people.

Put simply, to manage a home effectively managers need to be able to shape their staff teams in such a way as to influence their consistent practice, so that teams may in turn utilise coherent strategies, particularly in relation to the behaviour and education of young people.

What are the main implications here for practice, management, training and policy? Before moving on to discuss these areas, we provide a few words of caution. Research is inevitably limited to its brief, and, although we achieved our aims in terms of the design of the project, we are mindful that further research is merited in two aspects of the project.

First, there are issues concerned with costs. This study has carried out much needed exploratory economic analyses in terms of explaining variations in cost across children's homes, and differences in cost between local authority and non-statutory sector provision. The relatively small sample size means that statistical power has been lowered, and issues to do with accuracy of questionnaire completion and the like mean that we have to urge caution in relation to the findings.

In respect of insurance costs, high increases have formed part of contemporary debate (Gillen 2003) as being responsible for the closure of nonstatutory children's homes. In this research, we collected total annual recurrent costs of homes, which would include a figure for sufficient insurance cover as part of the operating costs. We are unable to report on the extent to which costs for insurance affect costs overall. Data on training costs associated with provision or with staff time, as well as sickness and overtime costs, were not covered in detail in this project, although staffing levels would account in part for time costs. Further and more detailed work would be useful here to enable us to debate the relative economic merits of each.

Reporting on the fact that resources do not have a significant impact on outcomes for young people provides an opportunity for misinterpretation to occur. There was no evidence that more expensive homes had better outcomes. We have shown that expenditure is not linked to outcomes; we have not presented evidence for spending less on the service. Other things, such as influential managers having 'effective' strategies for behaviour and education, as we have shown, matter more than expenditure. What is at issue is not reduction in expenditure or the closure of homes, but whether funds now spent might not be better used – for example, on staff selection, staff training and creating further homes.

Second, there is the issue of sampling. Recruitment in the independent sector was patchy, with notable enthusiasm for taking part in the work being matched if not outweighed by considerable indifference to it. Although we were gratified that many independent organisations replied keenly to our original invitation, the majority of those approached did not respond at all. The degree of choice experienced by organisations in the independent sector over whether to take part in the project means that those which took part need not be regarded necessarily as 'typical'. It is, however, possible to examine their contribution to see if some ways of running children's homes work better than others. Comparison between independent and local authority homes must be made in the light of this awareness. We need wider ranging research with a focus on non-statutory provision per se.

Bearing in mind these sensibilities, we turn to addressing the usefulness of our findings in relation to practice and its management, chiefly in terms of policy and training.

Implications for practice, policy and training

The ways in which managers work

Clearly, the way in which the role of manager is fulfilled is highly important. Formal standards and prescriptions go some way towards showing how to translate the role into the actual management of practice. There is, however, no single, clear, recipe for successfully performing the role. Its execution is best regarded as part of a social process, determined and negotiated contextually by those concerned. The precise quality of the relationships formed is heavily dependent on the creativity and resilience of the manager.

A number of issues relating to improvement are raised here for practice and policy. We are suggesting a critical re-examination of the following:

- Selection and appointment of managers. We have shown that some operate more effectively than others – clarity about what is required and how this is to be brought about needs to occur at the earliest point possible, i.e. at the time of appointment.

- Managerial supports. We have shown the disadvantages of acting positions, and that clarity in the role of manager is a pre-requisite of being able to bring about effective work (strategies). The status of positions and their purposes need to be articulated clearly at the level of the parent organisation.

- The ways in which formal support and supervision are provided for those managers in non-permanent positions. Currently, we have little information about the kinds of supervision that exists, its frequency or value.

- The way that support is provided for the role of manager over time, with emphasis on determining mutual clarity of roles, confidence in these and expectations surrounding them. As noted earlier, we have little insight into the process or value of supervision. Evidence from this study suggests that external support is often the sign of things not going well, is something that is supplied when a home is in difficulty, and is associated with poor outcomes. This alone suggests that there is a need for improvement in this area of practice.

- The ways in which the capacity of managers and staff is built upon and cultures are established, with special emphasis on supervision and training. Findings from the current study identify the importance for managers of getting their teams behind them, and some of the ways in which they can do this.

- The ways in which practice is monitored and endorsed, particularly with regard to risk and safe practice. One of the drivers for high staff ratios is almost certainly the wish to promote safe practice and guard against accusations of abuse. Any redistribution of resources is therefore likely to require alternative ways of ensuring these desirable ends.

Managing staff working in children's homes

We have seen that one of the main tasks for children's homes managers is creating and maintaining a staff team. Staff are crucial to what can be achieved by managers. While it is inevitable and desirable that managers play a large part in shaping the culture of their homes, and the shaping and organising of the approach to work that the staff group takes, this often involves working with staff who have little experience of residential care, or of child care. In effect, managers often find themselves in the situation of working with individual staff members in an apprentice-like manner, so the role becomes one which entails induction and education, in both skills and values. Although this has benefits in so far as it brings potential for positive influence on practice, there are disadvantages to this level of induction being required. The negative effects are potentially twofold.

The first issue relates to little to no supernumerary provision usually being made, so that initial 'training' becomes a hopeful event rather than an evenly paced induction where no drain on other members of the team occurs.

The second issue concerns the limitations of what is in effect 'on the job' training, where induction into working in a particular home may not necessarily provide sufficient breadth of approach for individual members of staff, and may in extreme situations serve to consolidate poor or perverse practice.

In the light of this, we suggest a critical re-examination of the following:

- The situation where staff begin work as a member of a team without prior experience or qualification. Potential for anxious, poor, unsafe or, at worst, damaging practice exists here, which places strains on everyone concerned.

- The status, experience and qualification of residential child care staff. Levels of pay, in terms of salary as distinct from wages earned by working overtime, should reflect the skills, experience and qualifications required. This has implications for human resource management overall (see next point).

- Staffing ratios. The study highlights the importance of practice and processes as distinct from high numbers of staff hours. This would indicate the need for appointment of experienced, confident and competent staff. Staff numbers, in turn, should be reconsidered.

- The dilemmas surrounding risk and the way it is managed within the bounds of good practice and procedural requirements.

Working for and on behalf of young people

We have seen the ways in which managers determine approaches to work with young people by taking account of the capabilities of their staff and spending time bringing about unity and consistency in approach. This was seen to be an evolving task, requiring reaffirmation over time, and varying according to the mix of staff and young people. Building relationships with young people with and through keyworkers and linkworkers is a necessary precondition for active work within the home and with networks external to the home. Relationships with field social workers and with schools and education departments are vital arenas in which negotiation and boundaries are dynamically drawn. Successfully establishing boundaries and routines for young people, and taking account of the needs of individuals as well as the group, requires careful collaboration, particularly in relation to bureaucratic requirements. None of these things can be achieved in short bursts of time. Pace is important.

The study also showed that increased lengths of stay in residential homes was significantly associated with lower total costs of care packages per resident per week and better outcomes. In addition, the potential for a home's lasting effect on the happiness of young people regressed to the mean after they had left the home.

In respect of these points, we are suggesting a critical re-examination of the following:

- What care in groups is able to achieve. The relative merits of providing highly individualised forms of care from within group settings need to be assessed. Where groups of young people are fragmented in order to achieve positive practice or calm atmospheres, the suitability of residential placements needs to be reassessed. Similarly where staff–resident ratios are determined in order to provide one-to-one care for young people, the purpose of the residential home placement needs to be reconsidered. The desocialising effects of long-term individualised care for young people living in group homes need to be investigated as a matter of priority.

- The duration of residential placements in terms of the relative merits of longer-term and shorter-term placements. We have provided evidence that higher turnover implies a higher cost per weekly place and also worse outcomes in certain respects. Conversely, stays in very high cost placements may be unaffordable – a point that further emphasises the need to look crucially at staffing ratios.

- The degrees of freedom around risk and associated procedural requirements. This relates to staffing ratios, which should be oriented towards improving experiences (processes) and outcomes, as distinct from oriented towards the likelihood of risk, or complaint.

- Strategies and support for ways of working with young people, particularly in terms of their behaviour and appropriate education. As we have seen, these are crucial in terms of outcomes.

- The relationship of residential care to what comes next for young people, whether this involves other forms of care or a move away from care, in order to maximise the benefits experienced while living in residential care. Our study is not alone in finding that improvements in successful outcomes are often eroded when the young person leaves the children's home.

Training overall

Each of these three sections raise certain issues that need to be addressed through training. It is important to specify what such training might entail, and how it might be delivered. Currently, we have little research which tells us about the forms, standards and merits of training that exists for managers and staff working, or about to work, in children's homes. We need to know more about the balance between attaining informative and detailed training and prescriptions which stifle the potential for cultural growth. Clearly these areas should be turned to as soon as possible in order to influence delivery and monitoring.

Given the importance of team work and team dynamics in children's homes, we suggest that certain forms of training should take account of the residential setting itself – that is, should be home- and group-oriented, with specific focus on individual context and purpose. Separate training programmes for managers should include a focus on individual and group child care as provided by groups of staff. Training experienced by individual staff should be oriented similarly to group provision. Furthermore, training in the home should be given due weight, with opportunities for individual learning being shared and appreciated by the group. Training should not be treated as a rushed event, which has to be fitted and juggled around returning to shifts.

In research terms, we know little about the fit between training and current practice or care standards. Similarly, little is known about where care standards sit in terms of the process of providing care or training for it, or the value of inspections in terms of the provision of care or, again, training for it. Once more, these are gaps in knowledge that merit further investigation.

Conclusion

The research on which this book is based has shown the strength of influence which the processes of providing residential care have for the kinds of outcomes that young people experience. In particular, we have been able to bring clarity to what leadership in children's homes entails, and what needs to happen for the role of children's homes manager to be performed well. Implicit throughout has been the concept of the group, whether in the form of staff teams or the resident group. To function effectively, managers need to take into account the strengths and apparent limitations of each group while working within their homes or across the boundaries of them. At the same time as requiring expertise in child development and in forming relationships, managers need to have skills in both individual and group work. We have seen that those working effectively must be able to balance the needs of the individual without fragmenting the group – that is to say, groups must be regarded as a core asset. Some managers of children's homes actively achieve this balance. A major challenge for the development of good residential care is to recognise and retain the benefits of group provision, without detracting from the individual needs of children and young people.

Our research has provided strong evidence that success in children's homes is not easily bought. The more expensive homes were no more successful in achieving good outcomes than the less expensive. By contrast, the project has shown that practice is important. Managers and staff working in children's homes where there were clear strategies for achieving reasonable behaviour and appropriate education were usually those where leadership roles were adopted from within collaborative cultures. To their absolute credit, such homes were able to achieve positive outcomes for young people. The challenge for line management and parent organisations lies in how these homes can be supported. The success of children's homes is increasingly dependent on it being regarded as a shared concern for all.

Appendix A

Research Methodology

As noted in Chapter 1, the research involved a quantitative study of 45 homes (30 local authority and 15 independent sector homes), a qualitative study of homes managers' roles, and a further qualitative study of a sub-sample of ten homes selected to present contrasts in resource use and leadership styles and characteristics. The homes and young people living in them were described at two points in time (T1 and T2), approximately a year apart. Information about the young people and the homes at these two points were related to variations in costs, size, the approach of the manager of the home and other factors likely to affect performance. The overall aim was to test our hypotheses through statistical techniques, through the analysis of concrete examples of practice, and through direct discussion of the conclusions with managers of homes and their staff groups.

Who took part in the research?

Initially we had planned to recruit five local authorities into the study but this number was increased to eight to achieve our total of 30 homes. Chartered Institute of Public Finance and Accountancy (CIPFA) returns for these authorities suggested widely differing costs of residential care. These eight provided us with local authority children's homes that were broadly comparable in terms of purpose and function. We also obtained from these local authorities lists of registered independent sector homes. Our target of 15 independent sector homes was achieved by approaching registered homes from within the local authority sample, and 'snowballing' (i.e. adding others from contacts identified by the registered homes) from there. This meant that, although we aimed here for similarity and therefore comparable homes, those from the independent sector were more varied both in terms of purpose and function and what might be referred to as 'company ethos'.

The recruitment of authorities and homes to the study was both time consuming and labour intensive. The study involved data collection from finance departments or their equivalent, field social workers, managers of children's homes, residential staff and young people. Each tier was approached directly and provided with project protocols and information, after necessary permissions were given from the relevant senior levels. This level of contact was essential for reasons associated with good research practice and ethical conduct. In addition, the initial stage of data collection involved postal questionnaire completion, and this may have been experienced as rather remote, depersonalised and lacking in relevance had not some form of personal contact been made.

Recruitment in the independent sector was patchy, with notable enthusiasm by some organisations outweighed by considerable indifference by others. Although we were gratified that many independent organisations replied keenly to our original invitation, the majority of those approached did not respond at all. The degree of choice experienced by organisations in the independent sector over whether to take part in the project meant that those which took part may not be regarded necessarily as 'typical'. However, it is possible to examine their contribution to see if some ways of running children's homes work better than others. Comparison between independent and local authority homes can be made only with caution.

There were a number of changes in those taking part during the course of the study. After T1 data collection, one authority withdrew on the grounds of organisational change, home closure and general overload. There was sample attrition of other forms, and many changes within the sample. Broadly, changes were related to organisational structure, the purpose and function of homes, and those appointed as managers of homes. All these variables formed part of the life blood of the project. Each change had its own impact on sample maintenance and commitment to the project. In consequence, a larger part of the research task than is usual was spent on retaining the profile of the project and keeping contact with those taking part, and this in turn had an impact on our timetables. We have captured some of the key changes in Table 2.10 in Chapter 2.

Data collection

Data collection involved three main stages. In Stage 1 there were postal surveys of staff, residents, managers of homes and social workers (T1). These were repeated in Stage 3 approximately a year later (T2). In the interim (Stage 2), and in some cases after this point, we carried out the collection of finance data. We also started, and where possible carried out, telephone interviews with managers of homes. The qualitative work in the ten selected homes began after the interviews with managers were completed. Homes in this sub-sample were selected to include a range of managers' experience and approaches, and a range of use of staffing resources – that is, staff hours, across the two sectors of provision. It was planned to include eight homes in this part of the study; numbers were increased in line with the number of organisations taking part, and in the interests of equity, as organisations were particularly keen to participate in this part of the project, the value of which was seen to be reciprocal.

The samples at Stage 1 were all the care staff (n=550), managers of homes (n=45) and residents (n=226) in the homes together with the residents' field social workers (see Chapter 2). Questionnaires were based on lengthier questionnaires used in a previous study with the same target groups (Sinclair and Gibbs 1998a). These questionnaires underwent considerable modification and piloting, in line with the emphasis of the current project. The postal questionnaire to young people, for example, was developed from what had been previously a face-to-face interview schedule. Considerable energy was directed towards designing and piloting a tool that was relatively easy to complete, took account of a wide range of literacy levels, yet yielded the necessary data. We negotiated support for young people's questionnaire completion should the need arise. We were keen that young people should have someone other than children's homes staff to turn to for clarification or literacy support. The kinds of people who provided support were children's rights workers and independent visitors. We did not want the questionnaire actively to be turned into an interview by the person providing support, as comparison of the experiences of the young people would have been made difficult. In effect, support beyond care staff themselves was taken up in very few locations. Young people were given an honorarium of £5 per completed questionnaire, paid in a form agreed in discussion with the staff and manager of the home, most usually a gift token of a conveniently located major store. Instruments were modified for the follow-up of young people who had left the home.

The samples in Stage 3 were managers of homes and residents in the homes at that time, the purpose being to repeat a measure of performance for the home. A judgement was made to omit children's homes staff from the T2 survey on the basis of setting their T1 response rates against labour and costs entailed in reminder phone calls and letters. Residents and social workers involved at T1 were included, the purpose here being to gain measures of change in individuals. Tracing the young people who had left the home since T1 was a complex task, which yielded 48 responses. Not all the 118 questionnaires mailed could be regarded as received by the young person intended, as destinations and present living circumstances were uncertain in a significant number of cases.

The interview topic guides with managers of homes were designed specifically for use as a telephone interview. This means had been used successfully in two previous studies by one of the authors (Sinclair, Gibbs and Hicks 2000; Whitaker *et al.* 1998) and is discussed in Chapter 3. The topic guides built on aspects from the two previous studies, and linked with the guides used with staff groups. The individual interviews established the manager's way of working in relation to key areas of practice, including resources; the group interviews identified the way that staff preferred things to work in relation to similar key arenas, and what helped this to be put in place, again including resources.

Economic data were collected via postal questionnaires sent to each of the managers and/or finance officers of the 45 homes participating in the study. Data to calculate the annual cost of the children's homes were collected using a questionnaire designed by Berridge *et al.* (2002). Data on the use of key external services were collected using a postal questionnaire designed for the purpose of the study but based on previous research (Byford *et al.* 1999). The questionnaire was completed by the managers of homes and included information on the use of health, education, voluntary, private and youth justice sector services over the previous three months.

Sample Models

The models discussed in this appendix are intended to show the shape of our analyses from Chapter 8. Those discussed, while not necessarily the most efficient, do give the main patterns of association. Rather than setting out the results of every multi-level analysis, we provide one as an example in Figure B.1.

Models for behaviour

These models were concerned with 'explaining' conviction or cautions for offences committed while in the home, running away from the home, and being excluded from school while in the home. A composite variable (deviant) reflected all these activities (one was added for each). The models discussed are based on a potential sample of 429 residents. This number, however, was reduced by including leadership variables in the equation as they were not available for four homes. The sample was further reduced by the fact that conviction was only an appropriate measure for young people aged ten or more and by some missing data on exclusion.

Even those who are used to multi-level models may not find the variables in Figure B1 immediately accessible. It is, however, useful to have the figure as an aid to explanation. The model shows that the likelihood of a conviction after arrival at the home is a function of length of stay (logged to reduce its lack of normality), evidence of previous exclusion from school and the degree to which the manager was rated as having a clear effective strategy for education and the management of behaviour (the strategy variable). The variable 'agefilte' gives the child's age but is missing when the child is aged ten or under. This has the effect of restricting the model to children aged 11 or over.

The next model was very similar to the previous one but dealt with exclusion from school after arrival. Previous convictions proved a more efficient predictor of exclusion than prior exclusion but even so its association with exclusion was not significant. Again there is a very strong association with strategy.

A third model dealt with the composite variable and contrasts with the previous two in that it treated the dependent variable as normally distributed rather than as one that only takes the values of 1 or 0. The model again included

$$\text{postcon}_{ij} \sim \text{Binomial (demon}_{ij}, \pi_{ij})$$
$$\text{postcon}_{ij} = \pi + e_{0ij}\text{bcons*}$$
$$\text{logit}(\pi_{ij}) = 0.709(0.147)\text{logstay}_{ij} + 1.036(0.317)\text{excludes2}_{ij} +$$
$$-1.206(1.020)\text{agefilte}_{ij} + -0.559(0.134)\text{strategy}_j$$

$$\text{bcons*} = \text{bcons}[\pi_{ij}(1 - \pi_{ij})/\text{denom}_{ij}]^{0.5}$$

$$[e_{0ij}] \sim (0, \Omega_e) : \Omega_e = [1.000(.000)]$$

Figure B.1 Likelihood of a conviction after arrival at the home

strategy and is very similar to the previous two. The next model dealt with the same outcome behaviour and includes the other three leadership variables. These were influence, management role and external support. None of them had significant associations with outcome if strategy was included (as a rule a coefficient is significant if it is greater than 1.96 when divided by the number in brackets – e.g. .385/.103=3.74 and highly significant). The relatively small (259) number of cases in use reflects the fact that only 40 homes had leadership variables and there were missing values for the component variables in 'deviant'.

Models for happiness and sense of well-being

These models were concerned with a resident's subjective 'happiness', well-being and feeling about the way their life was going. They were based on the 175 young people who answered the T1 questionnaire, although these numbers were again reduced when the four homes not rated for leadership were excluded and in two cases by the inclusion of a variable giving length of stay from another questionnaire.

The first of these models was concerned with the way young people placed themselves on a ladder where a high position meant 'high happiness'. The model shows that children who recounted a high number of pressures on them prior to arrival at the home were less likely to rate themselves as happy. They were also likely to have spent a comparatively long time in the home. Clear strategies were associated with good results in this model but – paradoxically – the manager's influence was negatively associated with outcome after strategies had been taken into account.

A further model examined resident 'self-esteem' but again proved paradoxical. It predicted our measure 'esteem', a variable concerned with the degree to which a child feels good about him- or herself and has a buoyant mood. The model suggests that homes do better on this variable when the manager has a clear role, and an official post. It also suggests that in these circumstances they do worse when they have a high degree of external support and are influential with their team.

A third model in this set was concerned with how the young person felt about their life overall. It is an example of a model in which there appeared to be virtually no variance at the level of the home.

Our final model in this set was concerned with the way the resident felt her or his life was going. This variable was related to the leadership variables but in a rather confusing way. Paradoxically influence and external support were negatively related to this outcome. Having a clear managerial role had a positive relationship with this outcome but strategy did not.

Models for residents' perceptions of home

These models were based on the same T1 questionnaire and dealt with how far the residents felt the home was seen as friendly, was 'well behaved', involved residents and had high morale. A final composite variable added these different perceptions together.

Perceptions of the home as friendly appeared to be influenced by pressure experienced before arrival in the home (the greater the pressure the less friendly the home was seen as being) and strategy. A further model was concerned with perceptions of behaviour in the home. It showed the familiar associations with previous pressure and strategy and a 'paradoxical' association with influence. Perceptions of resident involvement as we measured it differed very considerably between homes. They were 'paradoxically' related to external support – the greater the level the lower the involvement. Possible reasons for this are discussed in Chapter 8.

Our penultimate model in this set dealt with morale. After allowing for sex and previous pressure, the young people's perceptions of resident morale were not related to any leadership variable. Our final model dealt with the overall social climate, a variable formed by adding the scores for involvement, behaviour, morale and friendliness. It was predicted by previous pressure and strategy.

Model for psycho-social development

This model was concerned with a measure based on the social workers' perception of resident well-being. It was potentially available for 134 young people but numbers fell for the usual reasons. The model showed that our psycho-social development score was predicted by our score for the previous support they had received from their family and by the strategy score. Very little variation remained after we had taken these into account.

The next model dealt with the small number of cases (35) where we both had scores at two points in time and the young person was no longer in the home. It showed that where the young person moved to another location the strategy variable was negatively related to improvement on the psycho-social development score. The most likely explanation is that 'good strategy' improves the score but only temporarily. With movement the young person tends to return to previous status.

Model for staff perceptions of home

As described in Chapter 8, there were few strong associations between the leadership variables and the staff perceptions of resident social climate. Staff perceptions of the resident group as well behaved was related to the length of time they had been in post. This association dropped below significance if strategy was included in the equation (see earlier).

Models for staff perceptions of good induction, guidance on dealing with young people and general guidance

These models dealt with the degree to which the staff felt they had been well inducted into the job, had good general guidance and clear guidance on how to deal with the young people. Staff were more likely to feel that they had been well inducted if their induction had occurred recently and the manager had clear strategies. Their opinions of other aspects of guidance were also better if the manager had clear strategies but were not related to the individual characteristics (age, sex, time in residential work and in post) which we measured.

Models for delinquent behaviour including costs and sector

These models suggested that the addition of costs does not add to the ability to predict delinquent behaviour. Neither sector nor strategy was significantly associated with delinquent behaviour when put in together. Taken together, however, they do significantly reduce the unexplained variation. Moreover, strategy was significantly associated with outcome when put into the model on its own.

Happiness 'ladder', costs and sector

We carried out similar analyses for the 'happiness' variables. Costs were not significantly associated with the happiness 'ladder' in this model although the association was positive.

If costs and sector were entered together in this model, neither was individually significant. In this case, their joint contribution to reducing the variation falls just short of significance (chi square=5.896, df=1, p<.1). Both variables are, however, significantly associated with the outcome if entered on their own.

Social climate, costs and strategy

Costs were negatively but not significantly associated with the young people's overall perception of the home. The association between sector and this perception was not significant. The association strengthened if strategy was omitted (t=1.70) but remained below significance.

Resident psycho-social well-being, costs and sector

Neither sector nor costs were related to resident psycho-social well-being if allowance was made for strategy.

Staff perceptions of guidance and social climate, costs and sector

In general these models suggested that the private sector performed better in these respects but that there were no effects of costs. Neither strategy nor sector had significant associations with good induction if entered together. If either was entered singly, the association was significant. Sector is significantly associated with 'good guidance on handling the young person'. Strategy was not, unless it was entered without sector.

There was only one model in this set where we found an effect of costs and this was negative. The less good the general guidance was seen as being, the higher the costs. This association dropped below significance if strategy was taken into account. In this model, both strategy and sector predicted good guidance. Similar models entering costs and sector in an attempt to predict staff perceptions of the home showed no effects of costs. The independent sector in these models did better in relation to perceived behaviour and involvement.

References

Adoption and Children Act 2002. London: The Stationery Office.

Allen, C. and Beecham, J. (1993) 'Costing Services: Ideals and Reality.' In A. Netten and J. Beecham (eds) *Costing Community Care: Theory and Practice.* Aldershot: Avebury.

Allerhand, M., Weber, R. and Haug, M. (1966) *Adaptation and Adaptability.* New York, NY: Child Welfare League of America.

Argyris, C. and Schon, D. (eds) (1978) *Organizational Learning.* Cambridge, MA: Addison-Wesley.

Baldwin, N. (1990) *The Power to Care in Children's Homes: Experiences of Residential Workers.* Aldershot: Avebury.

Barber, J. and Thompson, S. (1998) 'Analysis and interpretation of cost data in randomised controlled trials: review of published studies.' *British Medical Journal 317,* 1195–1200.

Barriball, K., Christian, S., While, A. and Bergen, A. (1996) 'The telephone survey method: a discussion paper.' *Journal of Advanced Nursing 24,* 1, 115–121.

Barter, C., Renold, E., Berridge, D. and Cawson, C. (2004) *Peer Violence in Residential Child Care.* Basingstoke: Palgrave Macmillan.

Beecham, J. and Sinclair, I. (2007) *Costs and Outcomes in Children's Social Care. Messages From Research.* London: Jessica Kingsley Publishers.

Bennis, W. and Nanus, B. (1985) *Leaders: The Strategies for Taking Charge.* New York, NY: HarperCollins.

Berridge, D. (2002) 'Residential Care.' In D. McNeish, T. Newman and H. Roberts (eds) *What Works for Children?* Buckingham: Open University Press.

Berridge, D. and Brodie, I. (1998) *Children's Homes Revisited.* London: Jessica Kingsley Publishers.

Berridge, D., Beecham, J., Brodie, I., Cole, T. *et al.* (2002) *Costs and Consequences of Services for Troubled Adolescents: An Exploratory, Analytic Study.* Report to the Department of Health. Luton: University of Luton.

Blase, J. and Anderson, G. (1995) *The Micropolitics of Educational Leadership: From Control to Empowerment.* London: Cassell.

Blau, P. (1964) *Exchange and Power in Social Life.* New York, NY: Wiley.

Blough, D., Madden, C. and Hornbrook, M. (1999) 'Modeling risk using generalized linear models.' *Journal of Health Economics 18,* 153–171.

Brodie, I. (2001) *Children's Homes and School Exclusion: Redefining the Problem.* London: Jessica Kingsley Publishers.

Brody, S. (1976) *The Effectiveness of Sentencing: A Review of the Literature.* Home Office Research Study. London: HMSO.

Brown, E., Bullock, R., Hobson, C. and Little, M. (1998) *Making Residential Care Work: Structure and Culture in Children's Homes.* Aldershot: Ashgate.

Burns, J. (1978) *Leadership.* New York, NY: Harper and Row.

Bush, T. and Jackson, D. (2002) 'A Preparation for School Leadership. International Perspectives.' *Educational Management and Administration 30,* 4, 417–429.

Byford, S., Barber, J. and Harrington, R. (2001) 'Factors that influence the cost of caring for patients with severe psychotic illness. Results from the UK7000 trial.' *British Journal of Psychiatry 178,* 441–447.

Byford, S., Harrington, R., Torgerson, D., Kerfoot, M. *et al.* (1999) 'Cost-effectiveness analysis of a home-based social work intervention for young people and adolescents who have deliberately poisoned themselves: the results of a randomised controlled trial.' *British Journal of Psychiatry 174*, 56–62.

Cantril, H. (1965) *The Pattern of Human Concern.* New Brunswick, NJ: Rutgers University Press.

Care Standards Act 2000, Chapter 14. London: The Stationery Office.

Carr, E. and Worth, A. (2001) 'The use of the telephone interview for research.' *Journal of Research in Nursing 6*, 1, 511–524.

Carr-Hill, R., Dixon, P., Mannion, R., Rice, N. *et al.* (1997) *A Model of the Determinants of Expenditure on Young People's Personal Social Services.* Centre for Health Economics: University of York.

Children Act 1989. London: The Stationery Office.

Children Act 2004, Chapter 31. London: The Stationery Office.

Children (Leaving Care) Act 2000, Chapter 35. London: The Stationery Office.

CIPFA (Chartered Institute of Public Finance and Accountancy) (2000) *Education Statistics: 1999–2000 Actuals.* London: Chartered Institute of Public Finance and Accountancy.

CIPFA (2001) *The Health Services Database 2001.* London: CIPFA.

CIPFA (2002) *Personal Social Services: 2000–2001 Actuals.* London: CIPFA.

Clough, R. (2000) *The Practice of Residential Work.* Basingstoke: MacMillan.

Clough, R., Bullock, R. and Ward, A. (2006) *What Works in Residential Child Care. A Review of Research Evidence and the Practical Considerations.* London: National Children's Bureau.

Coates, R., Miller, A. and Ohlin, L. (1978) *Diversity in a Youth Correctional System.* Cambridge, MA: Ballinger.

Collett, D. (1994) *Modelling Survival Data in Medical Research.* London: Chapman and Hill.

Colton, M. (2002) 'Factors associated with abuse in residential child care institutions.' *Children and Society 16*, 33–44.

Crimmens, D. and Milligan, I. (2005) 'Residential Child Care: Becoming a Positive Choice.' In D. Crimmens and I. Milligan (eds) *Facing Forward: Residential Child Care in the 21st Century.* Lyme Regis: Russell House Publishing.

Curtis, L. and Netten, A. (2006) *Unit Costs of Health and Social Care.* Canterbury: Personal Social Services Research Unit, University of Kent.

Daft, R. and Huber, G. (1987) 'How organizations learn: a communication framework.' *Research in the Sociology of Organizations 5*, 1–36.

Department for Education and Skills (2003) *Every Child Matters: Change for Children.* London: The Stationery Office.

Department for Education and Skills (2006a) *Care Matters: Transforming the Lives of Children and Young People in Care.* Green Paper. Norwich: The Stationery Office.

Department for Education and Skills (2006b) *Children Looked After in England (Including Adoptions and Care Leavers), 2005–06.* Available at www.dfes.gov.uk/rsgateway/DB/SFR/s000691/index.shtml

Department of Health (1989) *The Care of Children: Principles and Practice in Regulations and Guidance.* London: HMSO.

Department of Health (1998) *Caring for Children Away from Home: Messages from Research.* Chichester: Wiley.

Department of Health (1999) *Me, Survive Out There? New Arrangements for Young People Living in and Leaving Care.* London: Department of Health.

Department of Health (2002) *Children's Homes: National Minimum Standards and Children's Homes Regulations.* London: The Stationery Office.

Dixon, J. and Stein, M. (2005) *Leaving Care: Throughcare and Aftercare in Scotland.* London: Jessica Kingsley Publishers.

Donabedian, A. (1966) 'Evaluating the quality of medical care.' *Millbank Memorial Fund Quarterly 44*, 2, 166–203.

Donabedian, A. (1980) *The Definition of Quality and Approaches to Its Assessment.* Ann Arbor, MI: Health Administration Press.

Donabedian, A. (1982) *The Criteria and Standards of Quality.* Ann Arbor, MI: Health Administration Press.

Donabedian, A. (1988) 'The quality of care: how can it be assessed?' *Journal of the American Medical Association 260*, 1743–1748.

Donabedian, A. (1993) 'Quality in health care: whose responsibility is it?' *American Journal of Medical Quality 8*, 2, 32–36.

Drummond, M., Sculpher, M., Torrance, G., O'Brien, B. and Stoddard, G. (2005) *Methods for the Economic Evaluation of Health Care Programmes* (3rd edition). Oxford: Oxford University Press.

Easterby-Smith, M., Burgoyne, J. and Araujo, L. (eds) (1999) *Organizational Learning and the Learning Organization: Developments in Theory and Practice.* London: Sage.

Efron, B. and Tibshirani, R. (1993) *An Introduction to the Bootstrap.* New York, NY: Chapman and Hill.

Farmer, E. and Pollock, S. (1998) *Substitute Care for Sexually Abused and Abusing Children.* Chichester: Wiley.

Finn, W., Hyslop, J. and Truman, C. (2000) *Mental Health, Multiple Needs and the Police.* London: Revolving Doors Agency.

Friman, P., Toner, C., Soper. S., Sinclair, J. and Shanahan, D. (1996) 'Maintaining placement for troubled and disruptive adolescents in voluntary residential care: the role of reduced youth-to-staff ratio.' *Journal of Child and Family Studies 5*, 3, 337–347.

General Social Care Council (July 2006) *Proposals to Register Domiciliary and Residential Social Care Workers in Adult and Children's Services.* Available at www.gscc.org.uk/NR/rdonlyres/193F9252-9E11-4FE4-8406-40D1432423A1/0/GSCCrecommendationstoGovernment.pdf

Gibbs, I. and Sinclair, I. (1998) 'Local authority and private children's homes: a comparison.' *Journal of Adolescence 21*, 4, 517–527.

Gibbs, I. and Sinclair, I. (1999) 'Treatment and treatment outcomes in children's homes.' *Child and Family Social Work 4*, 1–8.

Gibbs, I. and Sinclair, I. (2000) 'Bullying, sexual harassment and happiness in residential children's homes.' *Child Abuse Review 9*, 247–256.

Gillen, S. (2003) 'Residential homes desperate for help in face of rising insurance premiums.' *Community Care*, March 20–26, 20–21.

Goldstein, H. and Sammons, P. (1997) 'The influence of secondary and junior schools on sixteen year examination performance: a cross-classified multilevel analysis.' *School Effectiveness and School Improvement 8*, 219–230.

Gronn, P. (1999) *The Making of Educational Leaders.* London: Cassell.

Hallinger, P. and Heck, R. (1999) 'Can Leadership Enhance Effectiveness?' In T. Bush, L. Bell, R. Bolam, R. Glatte and P. Ribbens (eds) *Educational Management: Redefining Theory, Policy and Practice.* London: Paul Chapman.

Hersey, P. and Blanchard, K. (1988) *Management of Organizational Behaviour: Utilizing Human Resources.* Englewood Cliffs, NJ: Prentice Hall International.

Hicks, L., Archer, L. and Whitaker, D. (1998) 'The prevailing cultures and staff dynamics in children's homes: implications for training.' *Social Work Education 17*, 3, 361–373.

Hughes, D. (1988) 'A stochastic frontier cost function for residential child care provision.' *Journal of Applied Econometrics 3*, 3, 203–214.

Hunink, M., Glasziou, P., Siegel, J., Weeks, J. *et al.* (2001) *Decision Making in Health and Medicine.* Cambridge: Cambridge University Press.

Huxley, P., Evans, S., Burns, T., Fahy, T. and Green, J. (2001) 'Quality of life outcome in a randomized controlled trial of case management.' *Social Psychiatry and Psychiatric Epidemiology* 36, 249–255.

Jackson, S. and Martin, P. (1998) 'Surviving the care system: education and resilience?' *Journal of Adolescence 21*, 569–583.

Katz, D., Maccoby, N. and Morse, N. (1950) *Productivity, Supervision and Morale in an Office Situation.* Ann Arbor, MI: University of Michigan Institute for Social Research.

Kendrick, A. (2005) 'Social exclusion and social inclusion: themes and issues in residential child care.' In D. Crimmens and I. Milligan (eds) *Facing Forward: Residential Child Care in the 21st Century.* Lyme Regis: Russell House Publishing.

Kirkwood, A. (1993) *The Leicestershire Enquiry 1992.* Leicester: Leicestershire County Council.

Knapp, M. (1987) 'Private children's homes: an analysis of fee variations and a comparison with public sector costs.' *Policy and Politics 15*, 4, 221–234.

Knapp, M., Beecham, J., Anderson, J. and Dayson, D. (1990) 'The TAPS project. 3: Predicting the community costs of closing psychiatric hospitals.' *British Journal of Psychiatry 157*, 661–670.

Kouzes, J. and Posner, B. (1987) *The Leadership Challenge: How To Get Extraordinary Things Done in Organizations.* San Francisco, CA: Jossey-Bass.

Leigh, A. and Walters, M. (1998) *Effective Change: Twenty Ways to Make it Happen.* London: Institute of Personnel and Development.

Levy, A. and Kahan, B. (1991) *The Pindown Experience and the Protection of Children. The Report of the Staffordshire Child Care Inquiry 1990.* Stafford: Staffordshire County Council.

Leyland, A. and Goldstein, H. (eds) (2001) *Multilevel Modelling of Health Statistics.* Chichester: Wiley.

Likert, R. (1961) *New Patterns of Management.* New York, NY: McGraw Hill.

Lipton, D., Martinson, R. and Wilks, J. (1975) *Effectiveness of Correctional Treatment: A Survey of Treatment Evaluation Studies.* Springfield, MA: Praeger.

Mainey, A., and Crimmens, D. (eds) (2006) *Fit for the Future? Residential Child Care in the United Kingdom.* London: National Children's Bureau.

Marsick, V. and Watkins, K. (1990) *Informal and Incidental Learning.* London: Routledge and Kegan Paul.

Martinson, R. (1974) 'What works? Questions and answers about prison reform.' *The Public Interest 23*, 22–54.

Mellor, A. (1990) *Bullying in Scottish Secondary Schools.* SCRE Spotlights 23. Edinburgh: The Scottish Council for Research in Education.

Mintzberg, H. (1977) 'The manager's job: folklore and fact.' *Harvard Business Review 55*, 4, July–August, 49–61.

Mortimore, P., Gopinathan, S., Leo, E., Myers, K. *et al.* (2000) *The Culture of Change: Comparative Case Studies of Improving Schools in Singapore and London.* London: Institute of Education.

Netten, A., Rees, T. and Harrison, G. (2001) *Unit Costs of Health and Social Care.* Canterbury: Personal Social Services Research Unit, University of Kent.

Oliver, J., Huxley, P., Bridges, K. and Mohamad, H. (1996) *Quality of Life and Mental Health Services.* London: Routledge and Kegan Paul.

Oliver, J., Huxley, P., Priebe, S. and Kaiser, W. (1997) 'Measuring quality of life of severely mentally ill people using the *Lancashire Quality of Life Profile.*' *Social Psychiatry and Psychiatric Epidemiology 32*, 76–83.

Parker, R., Ward, H., Jackson, S., Aldgate, J. and Wedge, P. (eds) (1991) *Looking After Children: Assessing Outcomes in Child Care.* London: HMSO.

Patton, M. (1980) *Qualitative Evaluation and Research Methods.* London: Sage.

Rasbash, J., Steele, F., Browne, W. and Prosser, B. (2004) *A User's Guide to MLwiN Version 2.* London: Institute of Education, University of London.

Rice, N. and Jones, A. (1997) 'Multilevel models and health economics.' *Health Economics 6,* 561–575.

Rowe, J., Hundleby, M. and Garnett, L. (1989) *Child Care Now: A Survey of Placement Patterns (Research Series 6).* London: British Agencies for Adoption and Fostering.

Rubin, H.J. and Rubin, I.S. (2005) *Qualitative Interviewing: The Art of Hearing Data.* Thousand Oaks, CA: Sage.

Sammons, P., Thomas, S. and Mortimore, P. (1997) *Forging Links: Effective Schools and Effective Departments.* London: Paul Chapman.

Seale, C. (1999) *The Quality of Qualitative Research.* London: Sage.

Sefton, T., Byford, S., McDaid, D., Hills, J. and Knapp, M. (2002) *Making the Most of It. Economic Evaluation in the Social Welfare Field.* York: Joseph Rowntree Foundation, York Publishing Services.

Senge, P. (1990) *The Fifth Discipline: The Art and Practice of the Learning Organization.* New York, NY: Doubleday/Currency.

Sergiovanni, T. (1995) *The Headteachership: A Reflective Practice Perspective.* Boston, MA: Allyn and Bacon.

Sinclair, I. (1971) *Hostels for Probationers.* London: HMSO.

Sinclair, I. (1975) 'The Influence of Wardens and Matrons on Probation Hostels.' In J. Tizard, I. Sinclair and R. Clarke (eds) *Varieties of Residential Experience.* London: Routledge and Kegan Paul.

Sinclair, I. and Gibbs, I. (1998a) *Children's Homes: A Study in Diversity.* Chichester: Wiley.

Sinclair, I. and Gibbs, I. (1998b) 'Measuring the turbulence of English children's homes.' *Children and Youth Services Review 21,* 1, 57–64.

Sinclair, I., Gibbs, I. and Hicks, L. (2000) *The Management and Effectiveness of the Home Care Service.* York: Social Work Research and Development Unit, University of York.

Social Exclusion Unit (2003) *A Better Education for Children in Care.* London: Social Exclusion Unit.

Social Research Association (2003) *Ethical Guidelines.* Available at www.the-sra.org.uk/ documents/ pdfs/ ethics03.pdf

Starratt, R. (1995) *Leaders with Vision: The Quest for School Renewal.* Thousand Oaks, CA: Corwin Press.

Stein, M. (1990) *Living Out of Care.* Barkingside: Barnardo's.

Stein, M. (2006) 'Missing year of abuse in children's homes.' *Child and Family Social Work 11,* 11–21.

Strauss, A. (1987) *Qualitative Analysis for Social Scientists.* Cambridge: Cambridge University Press.

Taylor, D. and Alpert, S. (1973) *Continuity and Support Following Residential Treatment.* New York, NY: Child Welfare League of America.

Teddlie, C. and Reynolds, D. (eds) (2000) *The International Handbook of School Effectiveness Research.* London: Falmer Press.

Tizard, B. (1975) 'Varieties of Residential Nursery Experience.' In J. Tizard, I. Sinclair and R. Clarke (eds), *Varieties of Residential Experience.* London: Routledge and Kegan Paul.

Training Organisation for the Personal Social Services (TOPSS) (2003) *National Occupational Standards for Registered Managers (Child Care).* England: TOPSS.

Utting, W. (1991) *Children in the Public Care.* London: HMSO.

Utting, W. (1997) *People Like Us: Report of the Review of Safeguards for Children Living Away from Home.* London: Department of Health and the Welsh Office.

Wallace, M. (2001) 'Sharing leadership of schools through teamwork: a justifiable risk?' *Educational Management and Administration 29*, 2, 153–167.

Wallace, M. and Huckman, L. (1996) 'Senior management teams in large primary schools: a headteacher's solution to the complexities of post-reform management?' *School Organisation 16*, 3, 309–323.

Wallace, M. and Huckman, L. (1999) *Senior Management Teams in Primary Schools: The Quest for Synergy.* London: Routledge and Kegan Paul.

Ward, A. (2007) 'Working in Group Care.' *Social Work and Social Care in Residential and Day Care Settings.* Bristol: British Association of Social Workers/Policy Press.

Ward, H. (ed.) (1995) *Looking After Children: Research into Practice.* London: HMSO.

Waterhouse, S. (1997) *The Organisation of Fostering Services: A Study of the Arrangements for the Delivery of Fostering Services in England.* London: National Foster Care Association.

Whipp, R., Kirkpatrick, I. and Kitchener, M. (2005) *Managing Residential Childcare: A Managed Service.* Basingstoke: Palgrave Macmillan.

Whitaker, D., Archer, L. and Hicks, L. (1998) *Working in Children's Homes: Challenges and Complexities.* Chichester: Wiley.

Subject Index

Author Index